D1755769

THE HIBISCUS
Queen of Tropical Flowers

THE HIBISCUS
Queen of Tropical Flowers

CHIN HOONG FONG
M. AGRIC. SC., PH. D. (MELB.), F.I. BIOL.
PROFESSOR
AGRONOMY AND HORTICULTURE DEPARTMENT
UNIVERSITI PERTANIAN MALAYSIA

TROPICAL PRESS SDN. BHD.
29 JALAN RIONG
59100 KUALA LUMPUR
MALAYSIA

Copyright © 1986
TROPICAL PRESS SDN. BHD.
29 JALAN RIONG
59100 KUALA LUMPUR
MALAYSIA

First published 1986

ISBN 967-73-0021-0

TYPESET, COLOUR SEPARATED,
PRINTED AND BOUND BY ART PRINTING WORKS SDN. BHD.
29, JALAN RIONG, 59100 KUALA LUMPUR, MALAYSIA

Contents

Preface	ix
Introduction	1
History and Botanical Description	5
In Honour of Hibiscus	15
Uses of Hibiscus	25
Hibiscus Species	39
Hibiscus Hybrids	63
Propagation, Planting and Maintenance	137
References	148
Index	149

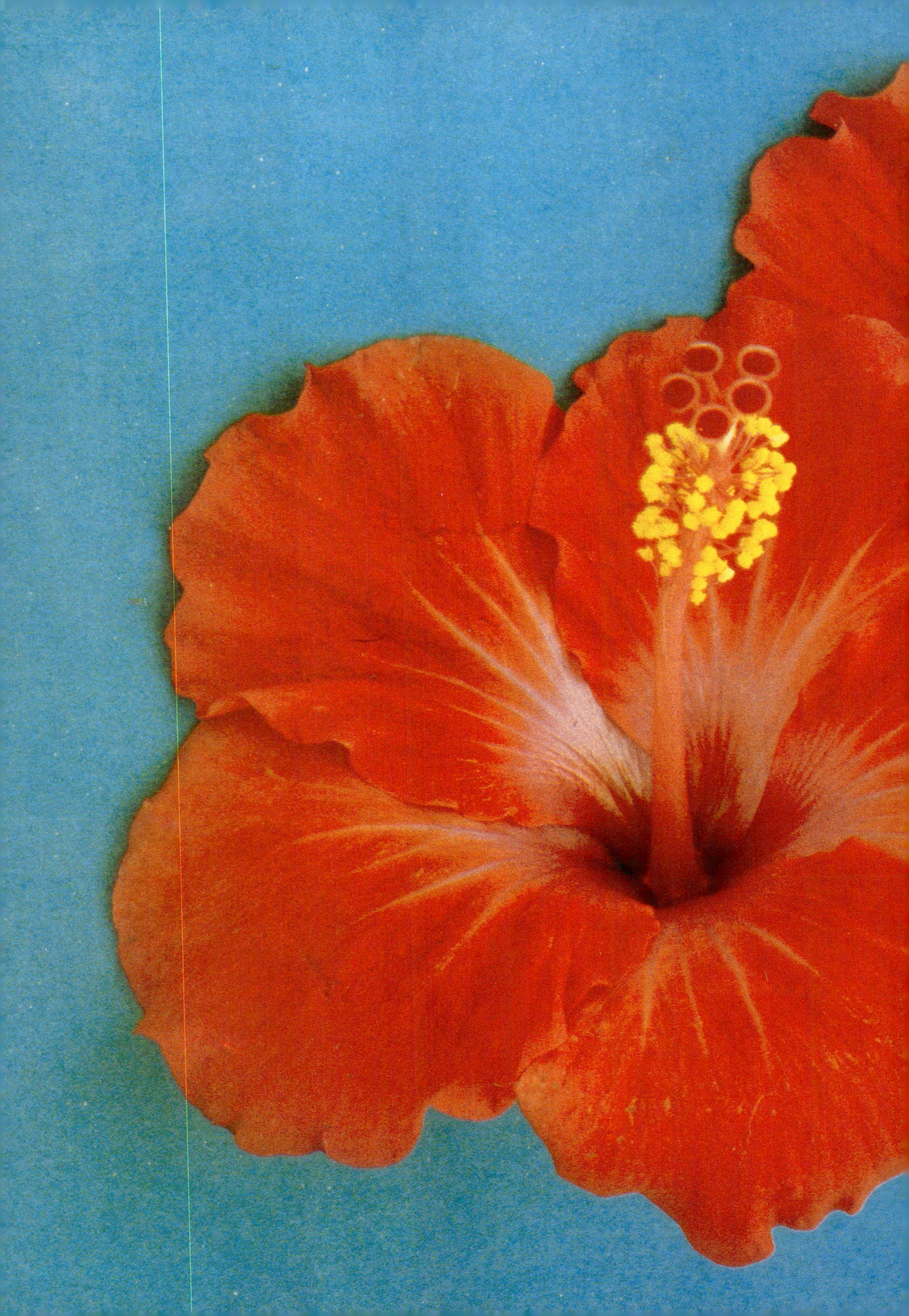

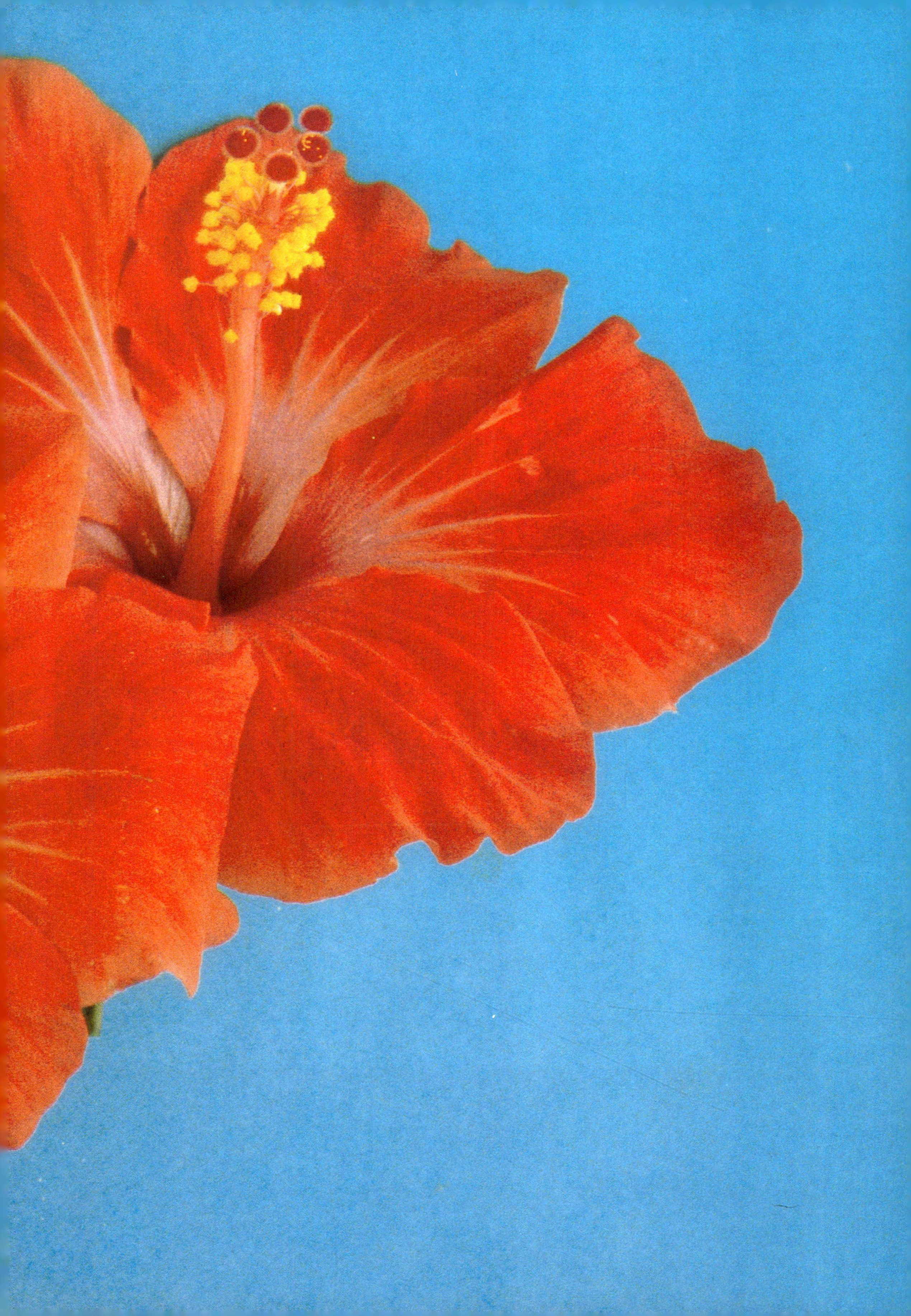

Hibiscus—Our National Flower

In the tropics the beautiful Hibiscus flourishes in abundance—
The magnificent blooms, a symbol of significance.
In Malaysia Bunga Raya is the common name;
With Independence came national fame.

Though usually large and red,
Other varieties in hundreds have been bred,
Sharing one common feature of petals and sepals in fives,
In a medley of colours and shapes to brighten our lives.

The formation in fives symbolizes the nation's five principles—
We obey and observe these ideals as disciples:
Belief in God, loyalty to king and country,
Upholding the constitution, the rule of law, and good behaviour and morality.

Each petal represents one principle in its entity,
Five fused together at the base to maintain unity.
At sunset the blossoms drop and fade away;
Comes dawn and new blooms start the day.

Hibiscus of numerous varieties have gained great popularity;
Soon our capital, Kuala Lumpur, will become the Hibiscus City,
Truly signifying the land of great diversity and beauty—
This heritage must surely be preserved for posterity.

Preface

The common hibiscus is well known to the world by many names, and has been crowned as the 'Queen of Tropical Flowers'. In spite of its popularity very little has been published about it as compared to the hundreds of books on orchids and roses. To date there is only a handful of bulletins, leaflets, and books on hibiscus published by the various Hibiscus Societies. This book aims to further popularise the hibiscus by illustrating its many virtues, such as its diversity in forms, shapes, sizes, and colours, with nearly a hundred colour plates. It also outlines the uses of hibiscus for landscaping and floral decoration. For enthusiastic gardeners, a chapter is devoted to their propagation, planting, and maintenance. Thus, this illustrative book is of general use for gardeners, landscape architects, nurserymen, and students of horticultural science.

The author has over the past five years photographed the beautiful blooms he saw on his visit to the Waimea Arboretum and Botanical Garden in Hawaii; the Mount Cootha Botanical Garden in Brisbane, Australia; Bogor Botanic Gardens, Indonesia; Peradeniya Botanic Gardens, Sri Lanka; the Singapore Botanic Garden; Penang Botanic Garden; and private nurseries such as Ooi Leng Sun Orchid Nursery & Laboratory, in Malaysia.

I wish to thank the various gardens and nurseries for their co-operation and help, the Vice-Chancellor of Universiti Pertanian Malaysia, Professor Datuk Nayan bin Ariffin, for permission to publish this book, Mr. Ong Choon Hoe for proof-reading the text, and Mr. Gary Powell of Waimea Botanical Garden for the four slides of native Hawaiian species.

April, 1986   CHIN HOONG FONG

INTRODUCTION

1 Introduction

In the tropics hibiscus is a very well-known flowering plant equivalent in status to roses in the temperate countries. It has a very long history, dating back a few thousand years. At that time it was known as 'the Rose of China'. Today the common hibiscus, *Hibiscus rosa-sinensis* is found throughout the tropics all over the world. Although generally considered to be a native of continental tropical Asia, it has in fact spread far and wide from its place of origin in China. Hibiscus was first introduced into Europe in the eighteenth century, and the first attempt to breed it started a century ago in Chelsea, England. This was followed by the efforts of enthusiasts in Florida and Hawaii. Since then hundreds of varieties have been bred, and their popularity has gained momentum after the World War II. Hibiscus Societies, such as the American Hibiscus Society and others, have been established in various parts of the world. Because of the large number of hybrids or varieties, being released each year, it is difficult to keep track of them, and the nomenclature for these new hybrids has become a problem. The same hybrid may be called by different names in various countries.

The genus *Hibiscus* in the cotton family, Malvaceae, consists of about three hundred species. Many of them are useful as food crops, vegetables, ornamentals, fibres, medicine, and timber. When one talks of hibiscus, it is usually the ornamental hibiscus, *Hibiscus rosa-sinensis*, that is referred to. Hundreds of varieties of hibiscus are bred, with variation in forms, colours, and shapes of flowers and leaves, but all bear the same scientific name given by Linnaeus—*Hibiscus rosa-sinensis*. In addition, these beautiful hybrids are also known by their varietal names. They are often named after dignitaries, such as President John F. Kennedy and after royalty. Sometimes they are named after their breeders, such as Isobel Beard, or they may bear lovely and fanciful names like Sweet Heart, Mini Skirt, and Firedance.

The hibiscus in Malaysia is known as Bunga Raya. The common name in other languages differs between countries. In Malaysia, Bunga Raya grows luxuriantly throughout the country, finding its way into homes in rural and urban areas. It seems to thrive without much attention. It is a hardy plant with few problems. It flowers all the year round, and is found by the roadside and in villages. Now it has become a fashion to have them in gardens, parks, home gardens, hotels, and apartments. Bunga Raya has long been associated with traditional medicine. It has been used to treat a number of sicknesses. Ladies use it as a cosmetic to darken their eyebrows and hair. In spite of all these other uses, the real reason for its popularity lies in the beauty of the large blooms which can be found all the year round. The hibiscus has thus gained international repute, and has been chosen by some countries and States, such as Malaysia, Jamaica, and Hawaii, as their national or State flower. In its role as a national flower, it has been honoured in many ways. The hibiscus flower has appeared in stamps, crests, and banners. Poems have been written in its honour; it has been exalted in paintings and carvings; and souvenirs such as key rings and enamelled spoons have been produced to further promote the everlasting image of the hibiscus.

This book presents a brief history of the hibiscus plant and provides botanical descriptions of *Hibiscus rosa-sinensis* and other species of hibiscus. It also outlines some of the uses of various species. The majority of the illustrations portray some of the varieties available to gardeners, serving also as a reference for identification. Lastly, to further encourage the growing popularity of hibiscus, a brief outline of the essentials of propagation, planting, and maintenance is included. It is hoped that in the future, throughout the tropics, more hibiscus will be planted, so that garden cities will become hibiscus cities.

HISTORY AND BOTANICAL DESCRIPTION

2 *History and Botanical Description*

About ten species or kinds of hibiscus are grown in Malaysia for use as food, fibre, timber, and ornamental plants. The only one of the group which is commonly referred to or called by its generic name is the common hibiscus, which is *Hibiscus rosa-sinensis*. A hundred varieties or hybrids of this species have now been introduced into Malaysia. In this book the main emphasis is given to this hibiscus species; some description of 17 other hibiscus species will also be described and illustrated in Chapter 5; and 72 hybrids or varieties with only names in Chapter 6.

The genus *Hibiscus*, belonging to the cotton family Malvaceae, has been so commonly grown in gardens all over the world that its site of origin is lost. Most likely, it is from the Asian and the Pacific region. It is believed, however, that *Hibiscus* is a native of China and Cochin-China (Vietnam), as it is abundantly found in East Indies as well. In Chinese history, records in ancient writing and works of art inspired by the hibiscus are to be found. *Hibiscus rosa-sinensis* was first introduced into Europe in 1731, and just a century ago hybrids began to be produced in Chelsea, England. This was followed by the work of hybridizers in Florida and Hawaii. In the late nineteenth century, in Florida, there were only about ten varieties of hibiscus. By the early twentieth century, in Hawaii alone, over thirty varieties had been introduced. During the first quarter of the twentieth century, many varieties, with colours ranging from pink to orange and red, having flowers with single, semi-double, and double blooms came to be available. World War II delayed the progress of hybridizing. It was only after World War II that popularity has been regained, and many new varieties have been bred in the different tropical regions of the world, though mainly in Hawaii, Florida, and Queensland. The first Hibiscus Society was founded as early as 1911 in Hawaii. A larger Society, such as the American Hibiscus Society, co-ordinates the activities of the various State Societies. Since then, many other Societies have been established in different parts of the world.

Hibiscus rosa-sinensis L—the Bunga Raya, or Chinese Hibiscus, or Rose of China—is probably the most popular and widely-planted shrub in the tropical areas of the world. It is found throughout the tropics but can survive in temperate countries if grown in greenhouses during winter or spring. It varies from 2 to 10 metres in height (Plate 2.1). It is an evergreen, although some varieties have more leaves than others. The leaves are also very

PLATE 2.1 *Growth forms of the Hibiscus shrub*
  (a) Drooping type
  (b) Upright spreading type
  (c) Open-branched upright type

variable in shape and size: the shape can be long and narrow to almost round. Some have entire margins, and some have deeply-lobed or serrated margins. Many are bright, smooth, and shiny, and some are hairy and rough. Hibiscus leaves are mainly dark green, but variegated colours are also to be found. In Snow Flake, the entire leaf can be creamy white, and some plants have red leaves of various patterns (Plate 2.2).

Hibiscus is among the world's largest and most beautiful blossoms, growing to 25 cm in diameter. The flowers come in a medley of colours, but the four principal colours, in addition to white, are red, yellow, orange, and purple. There are however unlimited variations in shades of colours. The flowers come in three main shapes: funnel, saucer, and reflexed (Plate 2.3).

PLATE 2.2 *Variation in leaf types, shapes and colour*

Hibiscus also varies in form. Most common is the definite single, i.e., with five petals in one whorl, while others are multipetal, i.e., the double form. There is another in between, which is the semi-double group. In fact there is practically a very wide range of gradations between the single and double forms (Plate 2.4).

Nearly all hibiscus flowers open in the morning and begin to wilt in the afternoon, and will normally last only for a day. A few retain their flowers for two or three days. Hibiscus blooms all the year round but most plentifully during the time of vigorous growth. In temperate countries, it usually blooms during late spring and summer. Although hibiscus flowers last for only a day or two, there are always new buds that burst open to take over the next day, so much so that the plant is always flowering. The blooms, in spite of their short life span and the beauty they provide, are thus always to be seen.

Basically, the plan of the flower is in fives. For example, a single hibiscus has five petals, five stigmatic lobes, a five-celled ovary, five teeth on the calyx and five to the bracts or epicalyx. The numerous stamens are joined together to form the staminal column (Plate 2.5). The stamen is made up of the pollen sac, or anther, attached to the staminal column by a filament. The pollen grains will appear on the pollen sac at maturity, when it ruptures to release the pollen. The pollen grains are large spiny ball-like structures when examined under the microscope (Plate 2.6). When placed on the hairy and sticky stigmatic lobes they will fertilize the flowers, thus producing fruit and seeds within 5 to 7 weeks. In each fruit there may be a few to 20 seeds. These seeds vary in size from that of the seeds of okra, or Lady's finger, to that of a large pea. The colour of the seeds varies from grey to dark brown, and the seeds are often hairy (Plate 2.7). In the hot, wet, humid tropics, *Hibiscus rosa-sinensis* and a few other species do not set seeds at all. However, in temperate countries, where temperature, and humidity are lower, *Hibiscus rosa-sinensis* sets seeds quite readily. In such climates, hybrids are easily produced when two species or varieties are crossed. Breeding work in the humid tropics is still very difficult, so that most of the hybrids or varieties have to be introduced, except for some of the native species and a few food crops like okra (*Hibiscus esculentus*) and Roselle (*Hibiscus sabdariffa*).

PLATE 2.3 *Shapes of flowers*
(a) Funnel
(b) Saucer
(c) Reflexed

PLATE 2.4 *Forms of Hibiscus flowers*
  (a) Single
  (b) Semi-double
  (c) Double

PLATE 2.5 (a) Longitudinal section
(b) Parts of the Hibiscus flower

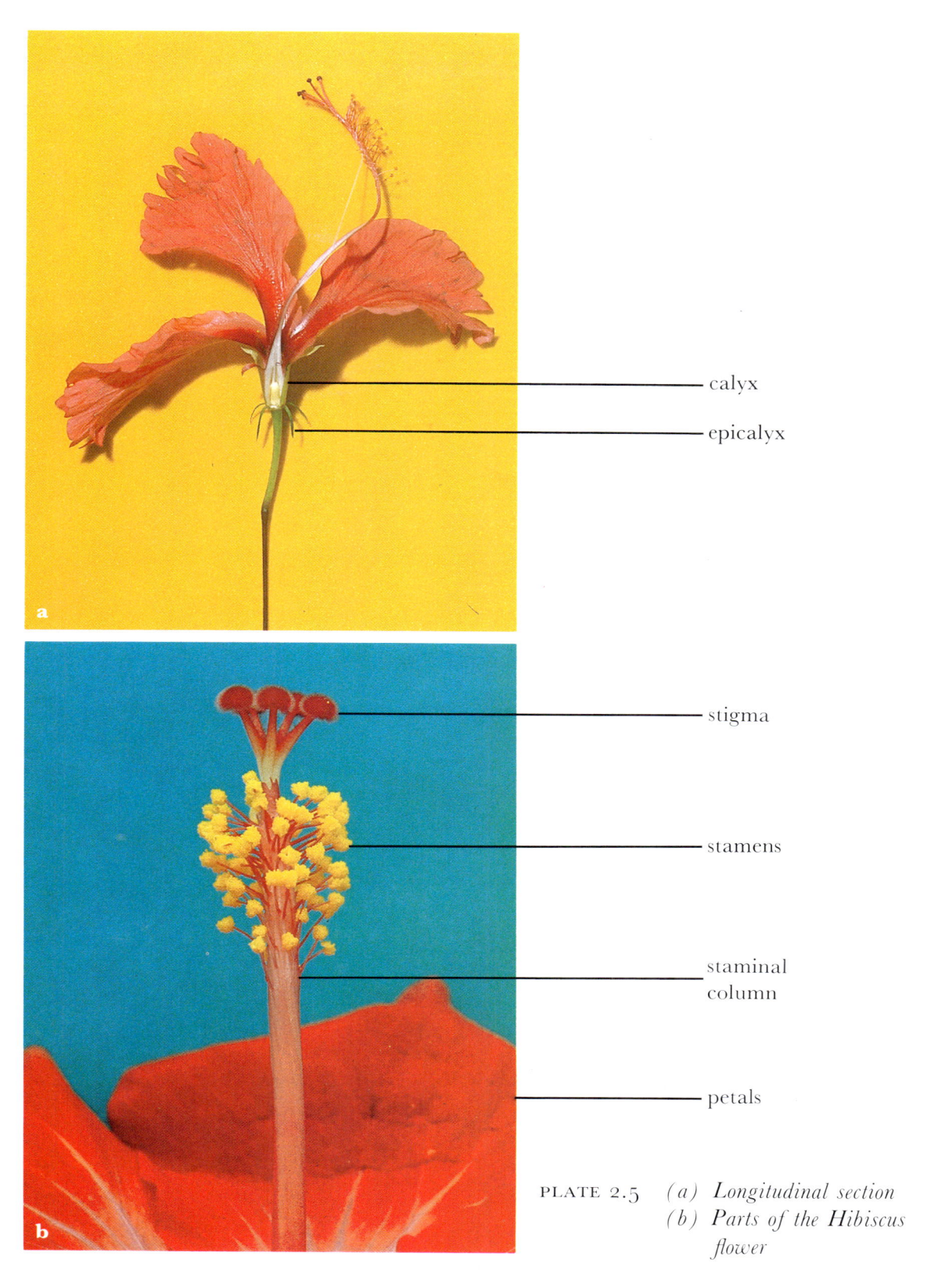

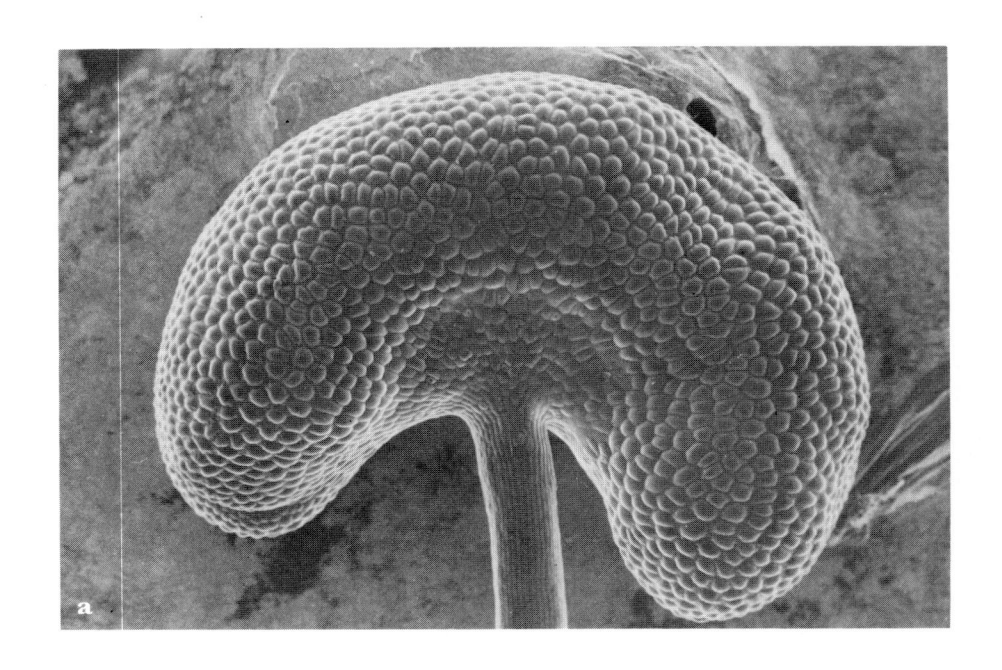

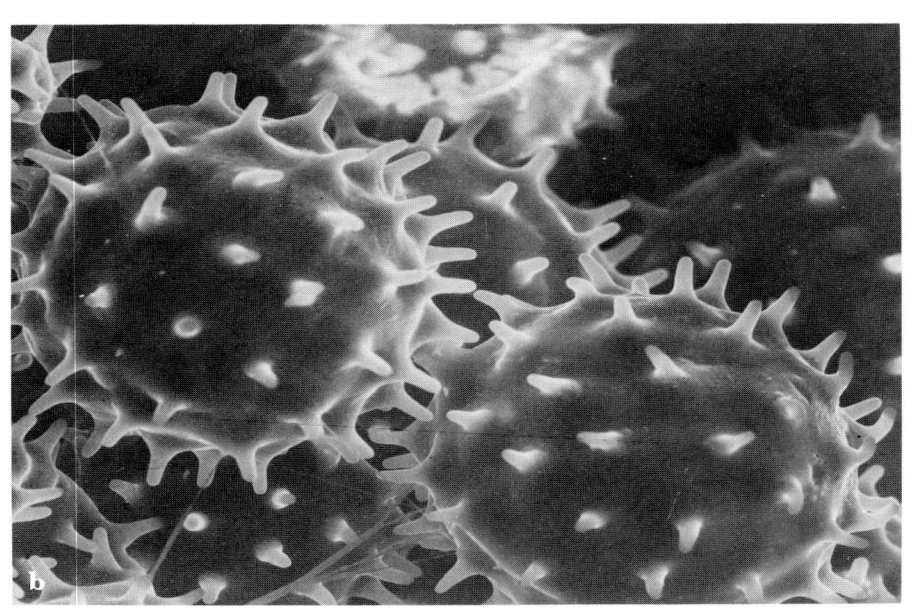

PLATE 2.6   *(a) Anther sac (b) Pollen grains*

PLATE 2.7   *Seeds of Hibiscus*

IN HONOUR OF HIBISCUS

3 In Honour of Hibiscus

Bunga Raya, the common red hibiscus, flourishes luxuriantly throughout Malaysia. In the past, the flowers were used as a dye. The juice from the flowers of hibiscus was used to polish shoes: hence, the common name, shoe flower. The different parts of the hibiscus plants, such as the leaves and roots, are also used in traditional medicine. The main reason for its introduction and popularity lies in the beauty of its large, attractive, colourful blooms, and also in its free-flowering habits throughout the year.

Today, Bunga Raya, or hibiscus, has been acknowledged and honoured as the national and State flower of a few countries and States. For example, *Hibiscus elatus*, a native of Jamaica has become Jamaica's national flower, while *Hibiscus rosa-sinensis* is the State flower of Hawaii and the national flower of Malaysia. After Independence or Merdeka, in Malaysia, the common hibiscus, *Hibiscus rosa-sinensis*, has been selected and named the national flower, and this brings national fame and significance to this common flower. Bunga Raya, today, is found all over the country: in villages, along streets and highways, in gardens, parks, the grounds of Parliament House, and in royal palaces.

Since Independence, Bunga Raya has received special attention. As the national flower, each of its five petals is interpreted as representing one of the five Rukun Negara (National Principles), these being: belief in God, loyalty to King and country, upholding the Constitution, the rule of law, and good behaviour and morality. As a symbol of national significance, the national flower has a place in many national organizations and even in commercial houses. Such organizations have crests, flags, and badges bearing the hibiscus flower. The Malaysian ten-ringgit currency note also depicts the Bunga Raya. Even a building and a road have been named after the flower, these being Wisma Bunga Raya and Jalan Bunga Raya respectively. In ceremonial functions and festive occasions, banners and buntings with the flower Bunga Raya on them decorate the streets, houses, and grandstands. This is especially so on Independence Day, in the Merdeka celebrations when the Federal capital is decorated by flags, banners, buntings, and illuminated coloured bulbs, arranged in the shape of the Bunga Raya. There are also fountains in the shape of the Bunga Raya, located in the heart of Kuala Lumpur. They take on a Fairyland appearance when illuminated at night.

Brochure for First Day cover

Hibiscus stamp

First Day cover

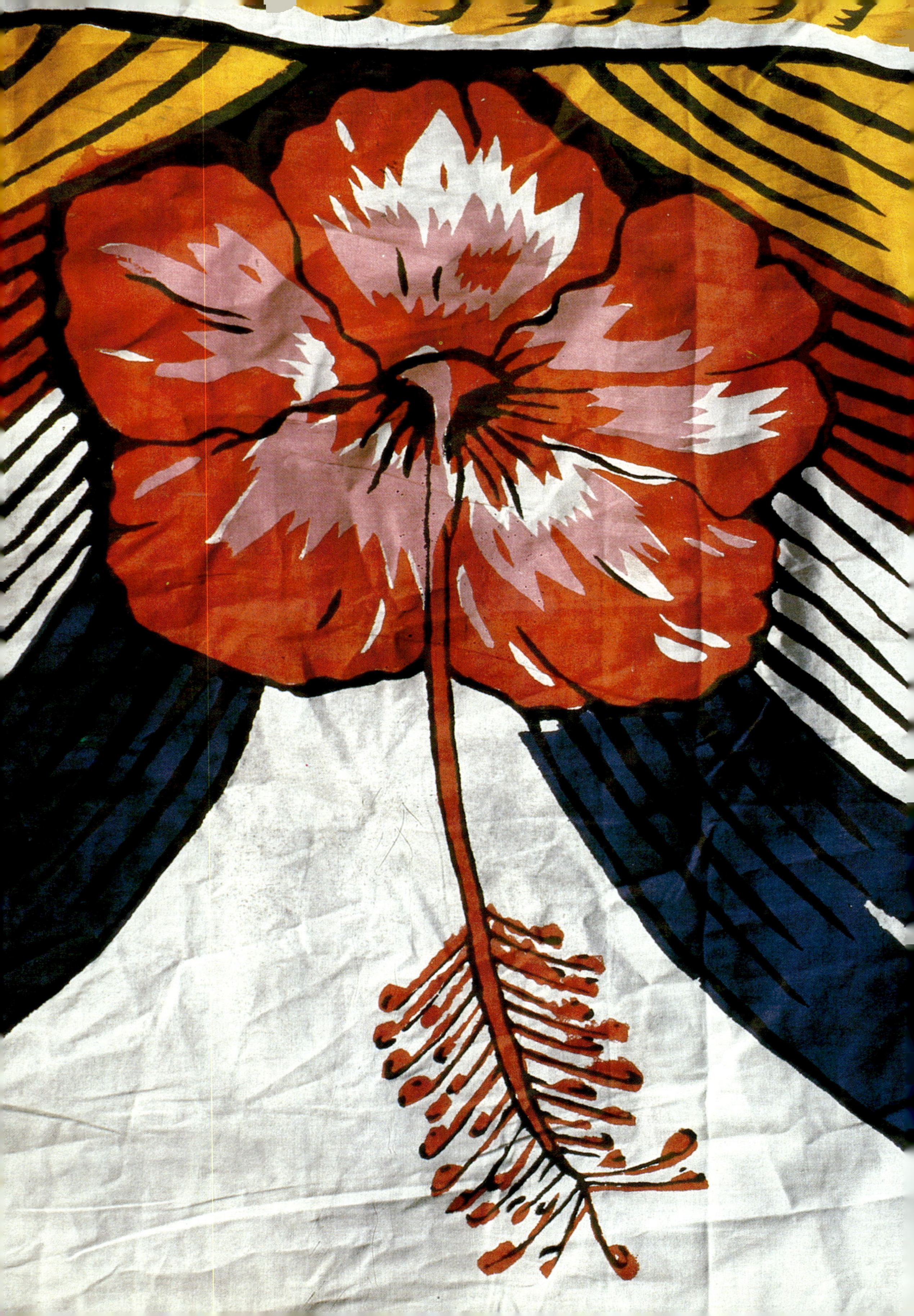

T-Shirt

Textile

*Calendar
of
Hibiscus*

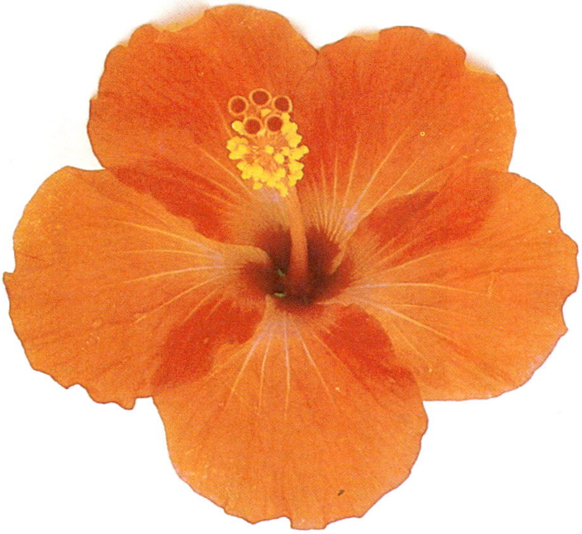

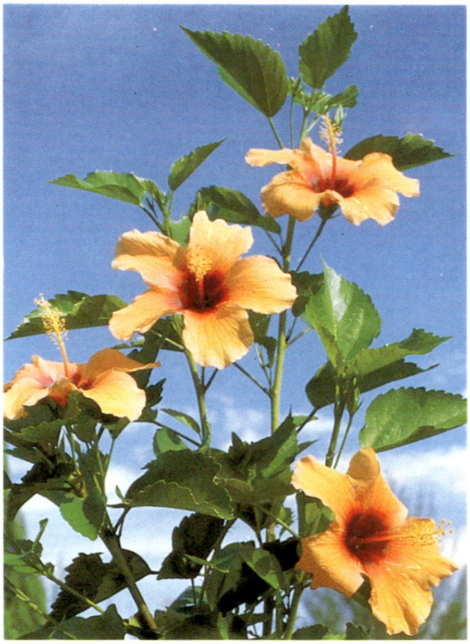

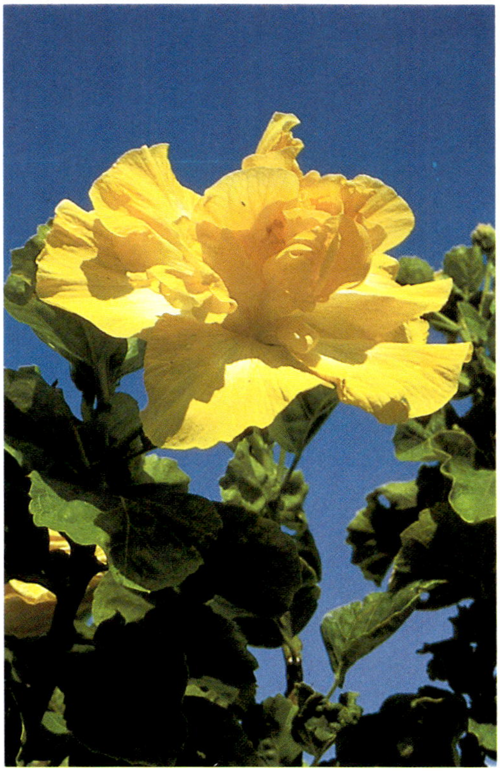

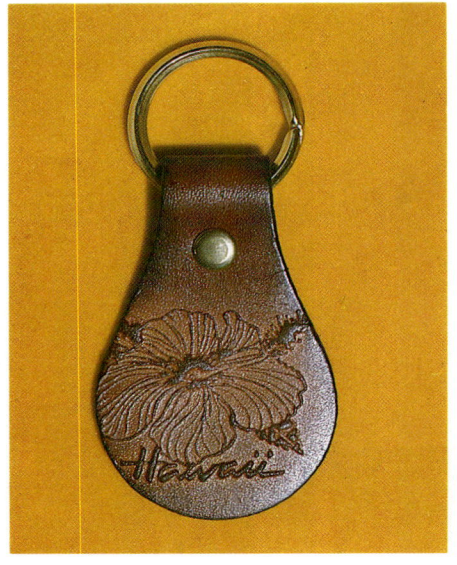

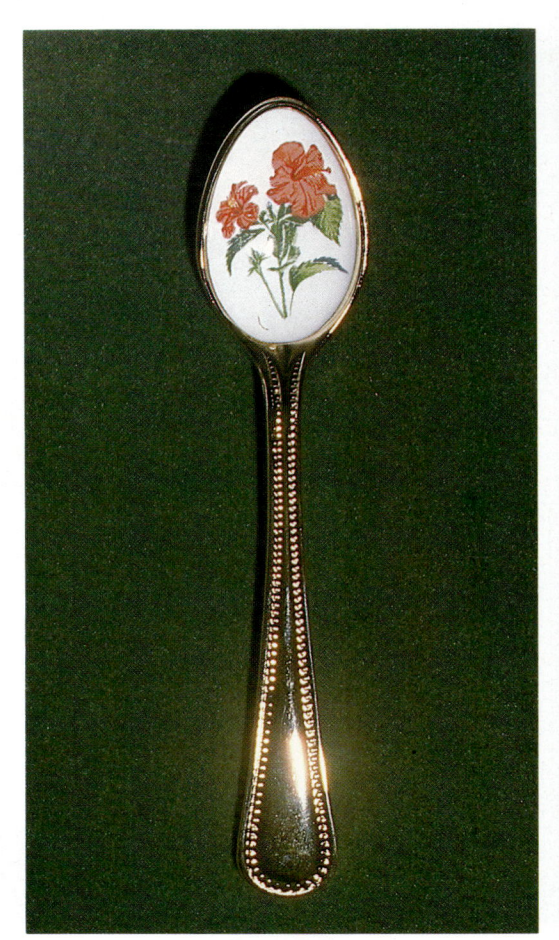

Key Ring *Spoon*

    To honour and commemorate its beauty, artists have drawn and painted the hibiscus flower in various shapes and sizes to be sold as valuable works of art. Photographs of hibiscus flowers and calendars bearing pictures of these flowers, are also common. Carvings of hibiscus on walls and staircases are to be found as works of art by sculptors. Souvenirs, such as enamelled spoons and key rings, are other examples of how the hibiscus is cherished by people from all walks of life. Lastly, the postal department of Malaysia has already put out two series of stamps depicting the hibiscus in the past, to publicise the national flower, and to give a national place of honour to the symbol of the five principles, or Rukun Negara, of Malaysia.

Shirt

Painting of Hibiscus

USES OF HIBISCUS

4 Uses of Hibiscus

The genus *Hibiscus* in the cotton family consists of about 300 species. The range of uses of this genus runs from shoe polish to food, such as vegetables, and drinks. The common hibiscus, *Hibiscus rosa-sinensis*, receives special attention in this book. However, mention is made of other species of hibiscus for various uses, including flower arrangement, and they are described in Chapter 5. They can be used for landscaping, ornamental work, vegetables, syrup, timber, and medicine.

Landscaping

The common hibiscus, with its many hundreds of hybrids and varieties, has become one of the most popular ornamental shrubs for landscape planting in places like Florida, Hawaii, and lately in Malaysia. Hibiscus flourishes in the tropics. It has attractive evergreen foliage and a long and almost continuous flowering season. There is a wide range of flower form and colour. These are the main factors contributing to its popularity in landscaping projects.

The City of Kuala Lumpur is to become a Hibiscus City. The City Council is planting tens of thousands of hibiscus plants all over the City. This is aimed at beautifying the streets, roundabouts, highways, gardens, and parks. Like the Hibiscus Garden in Waimea Arboretum and Botanical Garden in Hawaii, there will be a Hibiscus Garden in Kuala Lumpur.

Hibiscus is considered to be an excellent plant for landscaping, for it can be used for various purposes. It can be used as foundation or base plantings. Hibiscus can be planted on its own or in groups, as an individual specimen or as standards for formal use. On the other hand, an informal shrubbery border or a flower hedge is equally attractive. Variegated varieties, such as Snow Flake, add colour and contrast in group plantings. It must be noted that hibiscus performs best in full sun, but that in some varieties the colour of the flowers tends to fade when exposed to full sunlight. This should be taken into account when grouping the various varieties in a landscape.

At present, all over the world, in all new urban development, there is an ever-increasing awareness of the need for beautification programmes on the part of the community, the housing developers, and the town planners. Such programmes include planting in parks, streets, roadways, and highways. Hibiscus is excellent for these purposes and can be used to great advantage, especially in tropical regions of the world. Hibiscus can be specially beautiful when grown in combination with palms and many other ornamental trees. Today, hibiscus has become so popular that we can find it growing in many private and public gardens.

Pot or Container Plants

Hibiscus, besides being popular in landscape projects, has its place also as an ornamental plant in pots, in a small garden and even indoors. It does equally well in pots as standards. Each plant can be grafted with a number of other varieties to make it a unique plant which will attract a lot of attention. The potted plants, when in full bloom, can be taken indoors and placed in patios, the foyer, lounge, indoor gardens, or by the poolside, and they stand out prominently with their colourful big blooms. But the pots have to be brought outdoors regularly, by rotation with other plants in the garden, to get sufficient light for good growth, as hibiscus is not a truly indoor plant. Potted plants of hibiscus of various sizes can be obtained. They have a special place in roof gardens, in which they are exposed to full sun, and they are portable. Hibiscus plants in pots are also suitable for people living in apartments where space is lacking. They can be placed strategically in balconies, and shifted indoors as and when required.

Flower Decorations

Hibiscus blooms are well known for their attractiveness, but generally the blooms last only a day, except for some Hawaiian hybrids, which have flowers that remain quite fresh-looking for two, and in some cases even three days in or out of water. The work involved is compensated for by the shrub being able to produce high-quality blossoms all the year round. The hibiscus is not only useful for landscaping: the flowers have a place in decorations in the house when treated properly. The flowers have to be picked early in the morning and kept in a refrigerator without water, and they can then be used for flower arrangement in the evening. Some of them do not require water to retain their freshness, and these are best used with driftwood, palm spathes, and mats. They also combine well with fruits in table decorations. Even a single bloom in a glass vase can be attractive. One species of hibiscus that is of particular interest is the Rose of Sharon, or Changeable Rose. In the early morning, its flowers are pure white, but they change to pink by noon and light red in the evening. These white flowers can be picked in the morning and kept in the fridge. Just before dinner-time, they can be placed on the dining-table. Within an hour or two, the colour changes to pink, and this will certainly raise the curiosity of one's guests. The flowers will be the centre point for the evening's discussion.

Hibiscus, besides being used to decorate the home, is frequently used for corsages, both for evening and daytime wear. In Hawaii, many a lovely maiden (or even an elderly lady) adorns her hair with hibiscus blossoms. Garlands of hibiscus are used to beautify young maidens in the Pacific Islands.

Group Planting

Hedges

Highway

Parks

Food

The common hibiscus is edible, but it is used mainly for its medicinal value. One species, *Hibiscus esculentus*, commonly known as okra (Lady's finger) and locally called *bendi*, is used as a vegetable. Many varieties, of various sizes, shades of green, texture, and shape, are grown as vegetables which can either be eaten fresh or canned. The other edible species is *Hibiscus sabdariffa*, which is grown both for its fibre as well as for its fruits. The fruits have a fleshy calyx, which can be harvested and processed into a red sourish syrup used as a drink. In modern health food store, one can also get hibiscus tea.

Industrial Use

In the old days, the common hibiscus flower has been used as a dye. The juice of its flowers is used as a shoe polish: hence the name, shoe flower. The juice from the petals can be used to dye food, and also as a cosmetic to dye the eyebrows of ladies. It can also be used as a herbal shampoo and to keep the hair black at the same time.

Some hibiscus species grow to the size of a medium tree of 25 metres tall. One good example in Malaysia is Tutor (*Hibiscus macrophyllus*). The timber obtained from this species is of long fibre and good for making toys. It is soft creamish white in colour, and therefore can be stained or painted on. The bark of a few species, such as *Hibiscus sabdariffa* and *Hibiscus cannabinus*, can be used as fibre for ropes.

Medicinal Use

All hibiscus species are apparently non-poisonous, but some have a laxative effect. Various parts of the hibiscus plant are used for different ailments, depending on the species. These vary from the seeds to the flowers, leaves, and roots. For example, seeds of *Hibiscus abelmoschus* have been used in India as a tonic. The flowers of *Hibiscus mutabilis* are used by the Chinese for pulmonary complaints. The leaves can be applied to swellings.

The common hibiscus, Bunga Raya (*Hibiscus rosa-sinensis*), has its medicinal uses in Malaysia too. The Malays use a decoction of the root as an internal remedy. The roots of the red and white-flowered plants are used as an antidote for poisons. A decoction of the leaves is good for fever, according to Burkill, and a decoction of the flowers good for bronchitis. Preparations from both the leaves and roots can be used for the skin, and externally applied. The decoction of leaves as a lotion is used for relieving fever, and that of the leaves for headache, while that of the root may be used as eye drops for sore eyes. *Hibiscus tiliaceus*, or Bebaru, has medicinal value too. The roots are taken for fever. Young leaves are boiled with sugar and used for coughs and bronchitis in Java. Flowers boiled in milk are used in the Philippines for ear aches. Hibiscus is thus quite commonly used as a medicinal plant in the East.

Flower Arrangement

32

Floral Decoration

Standard Hibiscus Plants

Potted Plants

Single Specimen Plant

Hibiscus Girl

Flower Arrangement

HIBISCUS SPECIES

5 Hibiscus Species

The genus *Hibiscus* belongs to the same family as the cotton plant in the family, Malvaceae. In the genus *Hibiscus* there are about 300 species, consisting of ornamental plants, vegetables, medicinal plants, and forest trees. Therefore, there is great diversity in the shape and size of plants, ranging from a scrambling herb to a tall tree 30 metres in height.

In spite of these differences in habit, the common characteristics of this genus is that the leaves are arranged alternately. They are simple, and many are dissected or lobed, with leaf margin entire or variously serrated. They are normally dark green and shiny, but in some species they are hairy and in others with only the bottom leaf surface being hairy and variegated. Varieties with white, creamish pinkish, and red leaves exist.

The flowers are generally large, measuring 10 to 15 cm across. In some hybrids, they measure up to 30 cm in diameter. They are bisexual and regular, with parts usually in fives. The calyx is made up of five sepals, fused together to form a tube, and is subtended by an epicalyx which is characteristic of this genus. The corolla consists of five free petals, twisted in the bud stage. These petals also vary in shape, size, and colour. Very often, the basal part is of darker colour, giving the flower a dark eye in the centre. The male part of the flower consists of numerous stamens joined together to form the staminal column, which may be rigid or long and pendulous. At the tip of the column are five hairy stigmatic lobes, which are normally reddish, yellowish, or creamy in colour. The flower opens in the morning and fades away in the evening. Some may remain for two to three days. On successful pollination and fertilization, fruits are formed. The fruits are in the form of capsules or angular pods, opening when ripe to release the seeds. Seeds of hibiscus vary in size from that of a mungbean to that of a pea, each measuring from 0.3 cm to 1 cm across. Each fruit may contain a few to 20 seeds. The seed is greyish to dark brown in colour, and can be hairy, with markings like fingerprints (see Chapter 2). Hibiscus seeds are normally hard, and some are difficult to germinate, taking from 1 to 12 weeks. Hence they have to be scarified, or heat treated, before sowing.

Bunga Raya, Chinese Hibiscus or Rose, Shoe Flower
Hibiscus rosa-sinensis

The common hibiscus is an evergreen shrub, and grows to a height of 2 to 6 metres. The places of origin of this species are Asia and the Pacific.

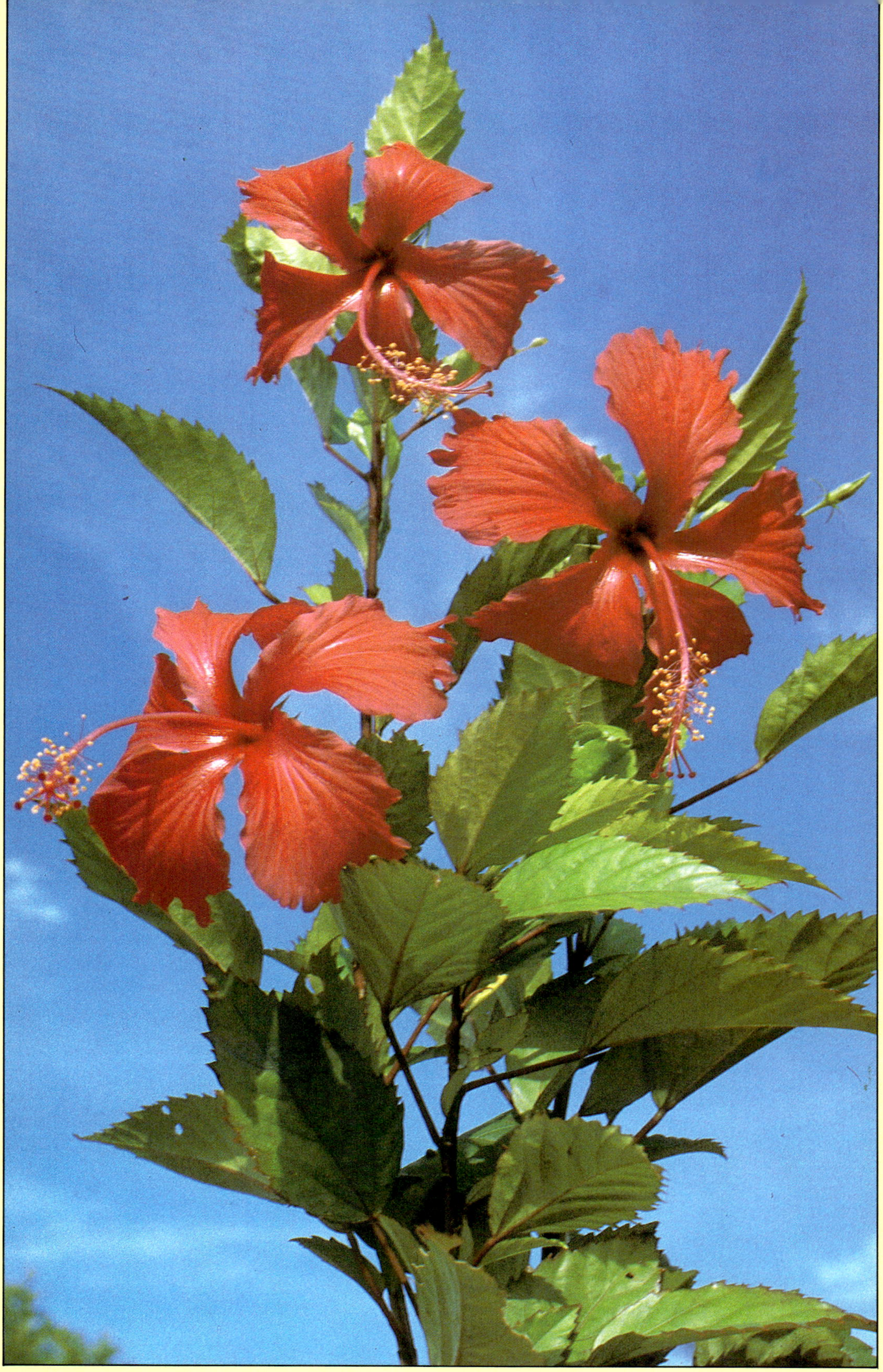

Bunga Raya, Shoe Flower
Hibiscus rosa-sinensis

However, it is believed to have originated in China and Cochin-China (Vietnam). It can be grown as a potted plant, a standard, or in groups, and even as hedges too. This plant possesses attractive, shiny, dark green leaves which are usually serrated. They make excellent potted plants, even for indoors, provided they are exposed to a maximum amount of sunlight and moderate temperature.

The hibiscus flowers all the year round in the tropics. The magnificent large blooms last only for a day or two, but as one fades away, another in the bud stage is ready to open. The flowers are either single, semi-double, or double, and come in a medley of colours ranging from pure white to dark red. The size of the flowers is considered to be large, the average measuring 15 cm across. The hybrids can measure up to 30 cm. Hundreds of hybrids and varieties have been bred and selected (see Chapter 6), with various shapes, sizes, and colours.

Hibiscus, besides its ornamental value, has many other uses, such as medicine, and cosmetics for dyeing the hair and eyebrows. The juice of the flowers can be used also as a shoe polish: hence the name, shoe flower.

Bunga Raya is locally propagated mainly by stem cuttings, grafting, and marcotting (see Chapter 7). In places like Hawaii, Florida, and Queensland, seeds are also used. In Malaysia, Bunga Raya does not set seeds.

Rose of Sharon, Cotton Rose Hibiscus, Changeable Rose Mallow
Hibiscus mutabilis

This plant has its origin in China and is now a common garden shrub all over the tropics. It is an evergreen species, growing to a height of 2 to 3 metres. The Rose of Sharon has hairy leaves, which are not bright and shiny as those of Bunga Raya. The most interesting feature of this species is that it produces large double flowers up to 10 cm across, and that the flowers are white when they open early in the morning. Soon they change to pink as the temperature rises in the afternoon, and finally they turn red in the evening before they fade away. This is how this species got the specific name *mutabilis*, which means changeable. This character renders it an interesting specimen for home decorations, especially for the dining table. Flowers can be harvested in the morning and kept in the fridge, and then displayed on the dining table at dinner time.

9.00AM

12.00N

3.00PM

The flowers will turn from white to pink over a period of an hour while the dinner is on.

This plant can be grown easily in the garden, providing continuous change of colour during the day. It is propagated easily by cuttings.

Lady's Finger, Okra, Bendi
Hibiscus esculentus

Originating in tropical Africa, the okra has spread widely throughout the tropics. An erect, robust, annual herb, it grows to 1 to 2 metres tall, and has green or red-tinged stems with alternate leaves, which are palmately 3–7-lobed and pale green beneath. The flowers are solitary and borne in the leaf axils, and yellow in colour with a crimson-spot centre. The fruits are used as vegetables. The ripe seeds contain 20% edible oil. The plant grows well in lowland tropics and best on well-manured loams. It is propagated mainly by seeds.

Musk Mallow, Musk Seed, Kapas Hutan

Hibiscus abelmoschus (H. Manihot)

A native of China, the Kapas Hutan is an erect, bristly herb, 1 to 1.5 metres in height. It has 3- to 5-lobed leaves which are oblong or linear and are 8 to 13 cm long. The flowers are 7 cm across, and yellow with a maroon crimson eye. The capsules are hairy and about 5 cm long. The seeds are musky-scented and have medicinal value. It is mainly grown from seeds.

Timur Hibiscus, Beach or Sea Hibiscus, Tree Hibiscus
Hibiscus tiliaceus

This is a hardy evergreen tree found along coastal areas of the tropics, mainly in Asia, Australia, and the Pacific. In Malaysia, it is commonly found on sandy and rocky shores. The tree has a short trunk and a spreading crown, and grows to 7 to 10 metres high. The flowers are large, yellow with a maroon centre, and are borne at the ends of branches. The flowers remain fresh for one or two days on the tree, turning orange red before falling to the ground. The tree has been used in street planting, but has to undergo careful pruning to get a good shape. The Sea Hibiscus can be propagated by seed, and preferably by 2-metre long cuttings. The tree has the advantage of rapid growth, and is wind- and salt-resistant. In Tahiti, the flowers are used as garlands, and the bark as fibre and cordage, and for caulking boats.

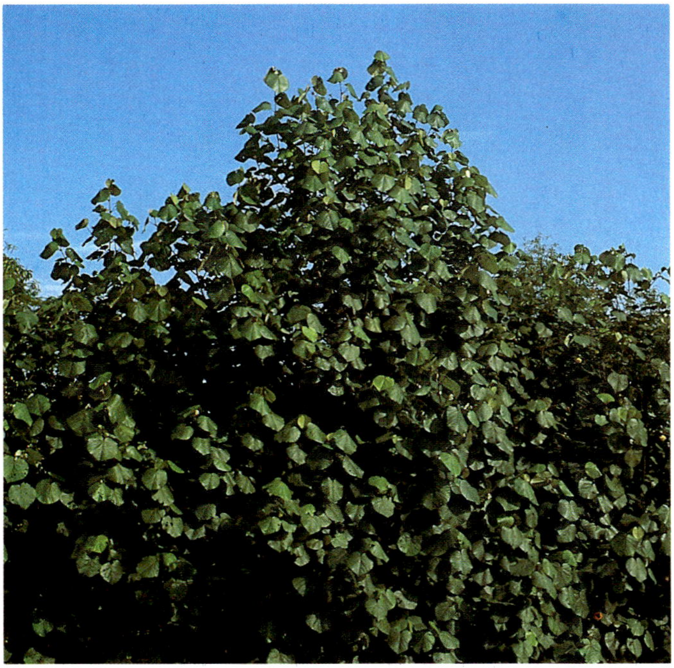

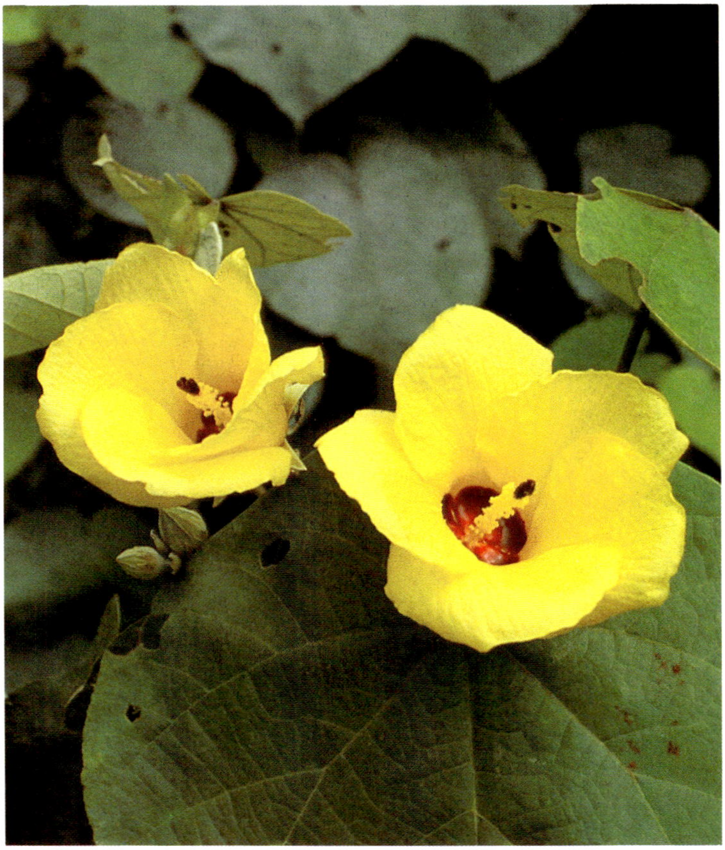

Coral Hibiscus, Japanese Lanterns
Hibiscus schizopetalus

The coral hibiscus originated from East Africa. Being a shrub, it grows to a height of about 4 metres. The leaves are shiny, and the leaf margin is serrated. The shrub produces delicate pendulous flowers, which hang from the axils of leaves like red lanterns. The flowers are bright red, measuring about 6 to 8 cm across the petals dissected and reflexed, thus showing off its long style, ending with five reddish stigmatic lobes. The coral hibiscus grows easily, and is common as an ornamental shrub in local home gardens. It grows well in full sunlight, and is propagated by cuttings and marcottings.

Syrian Ketrina
Hibiscus syriacus

This is a distinctive deciduous shrub, having its origin in South and East Asia, and grows to a height of 3 metres. The leaves are 4 to 7 cm long, three-lobed, and have star-shaped hairs beneath. The flowers are fairly large, and lilac or bluish in colour.

This species is widely grown as an ornamental plant and as a hedge plant in Southern Europe. Many cultivated forms are planted, showing a wide range of colour variations. The blue hibiscus (*Hibiscus syriacus*), coming in both single and double forms, does not adapt very well to the Malaysian climate, and rarely flowers. It needs a very well-drained soil, and is best grown in a pot. It is propagated by cuttings.

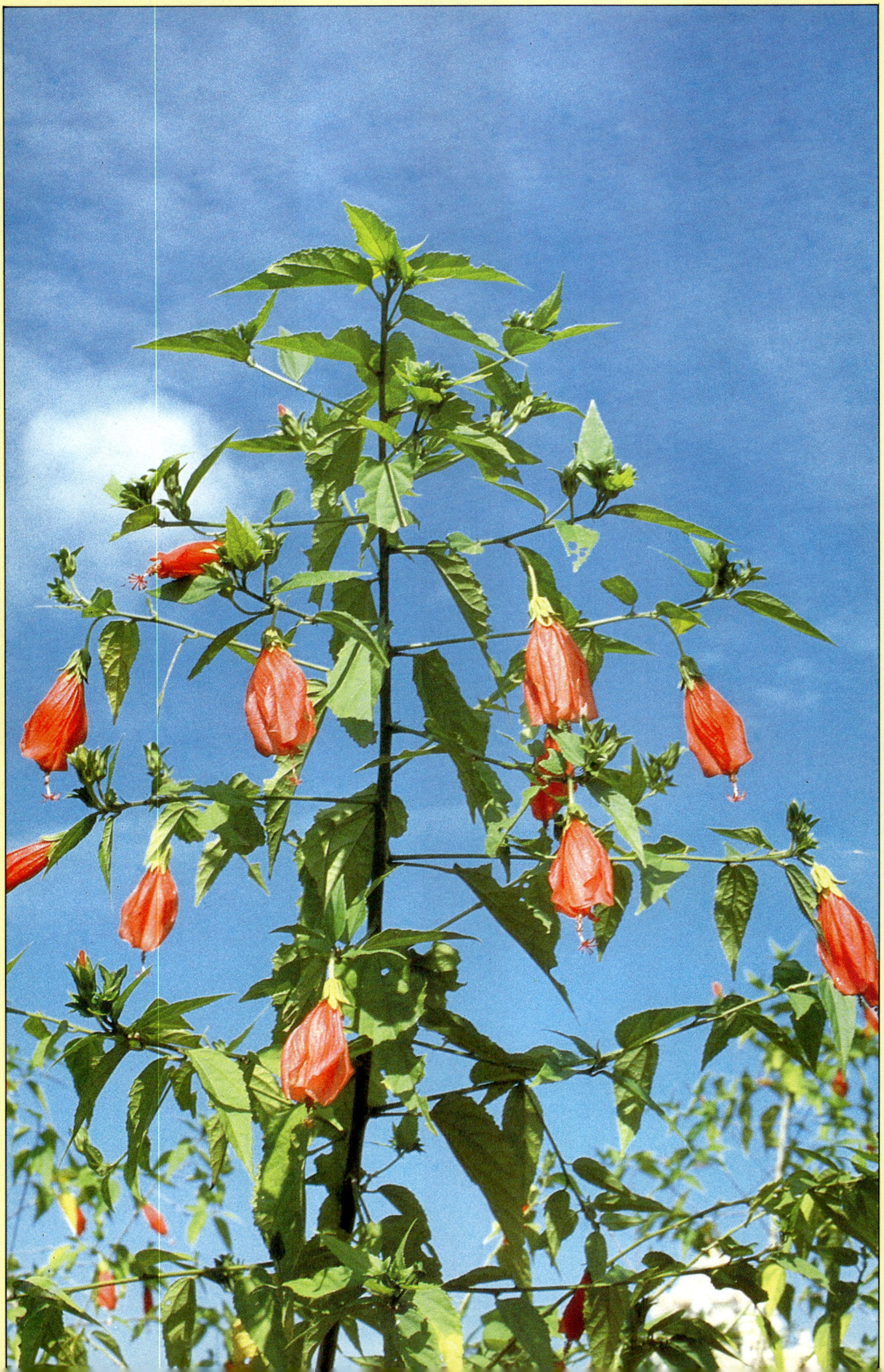

Turk's Cap

Malvaviscus conzatii

A tall shrub with open branching, this species looks very much like the hibiscus in both leaf and flower form. The only difference is that the flowers do not open fully. The flowers are either red or pink. The shrub is free-flowering. Usually it is used in mixed borders. It is propagated from cuttings.

Rose Mallow
Hibiscus moschentos

A native of Europe and Asia, the Rose Mallow is a narrow-growing perennial shrub with hairy leaves. It grows to a height of 1 to 2.5 metres. The flowers are large, 13 to 20 cm wide, and come in shades of pink, red, or white. It requires a rich, well-drained, moist soil, and light shade or full sun. Grown also as a hedge plant and as a cut flower, it can be propagated by seeds and cuttings.

Tutor

Hibiscus macrophyllus

Tutor is found commonly in the lowland forest and secondary jungles of Malaysia. It is a small to medium tree, up to 24 metres in height, and has an open crown. The timber obtained from this tree is creamish white, soft, and has long fibres. The wood is useful for making toys, and can be coloured readily. The fibres from the bark are used for ropes.

The leaves are very large, measuring 15 to 35 cm across and have a long petiole or leaf stalk up to 24 cm in length. They are roundish in shape, the apex ending abruptly with a long tip. The base of the leaf is heart-shaped. The leaf and stalk are hairy on both sides. The flowers are yellow and large, and are bell-shaped. The fruit measures about 2.5 cm wide, and bears many seeds which are also hairy. This species is easily propagated from seeds.

Roselle, Red Sorrel, Asam Susur
Hibiscus sabdariffa
The Roselle is an erect, glabrous, annual shrub, and is believed to have its origin in tropical Africa. It has been grown in India, Africa, and America since the eighteenth century. The shrub grows to 3 metres tall and has glabrous leaves, which are palmately lobed with serrated margins and which are carried on long petioles. The flowers are showy, and are borne singly on very short peduncles in the axils of the upper leaves. The calyces of the flowers are reddish and fleshy, and can be harvested and made into a red syrup for cold drinks. The seeds contain 17% oil similar in properties to cotton seed oil. The shrub is propagated by seeds.

57

Red-leaf Hibiscus
Hibiscus acetosella

This is a native of tropical Africa, but it is found quite commonly grown in home gardens in the United States and lately in Malaysia too. The Red-Leaf Hibiscus is a shrub growing to 2 to 3 metres tall. The leaves and stems are magenta red, but plants with light red leaves and stems are also to be found. The flowers are normally red, like those of the common hibiscus, but yellow and creamy coloured flowers are also found.

Rock's Hibiscus
Hibiscus rockii

Rock's Hibiscus is found in the island of Kauai, in Hawaii. It is a hairy shrub growing to 10 to 15 dm tall. The leaves are dull, especially the undersurface. The leaf shape is 3-lobed, and measures 8 cm long and 9 cm wide. The flowers open in the afternoon. Each is 10 cm wide, arising singly from the axils of lower leaves. They are yellow in colour, with a dark, reddish brown eye at the centre. The shrub sets fruits at maturity, producing seeds which are dark brown, each measuring 4.5 mm long and 3 mm wide. This species does well in shady areas and can be propagated by seeds or cuttings.

Pukoonis

Hibiscus kokio

A native of Hawaii, growing into a shrub and sometimes a straggly bush. It has a distinct growth form which is quite different from that of other varieties. The flowers average 7.5 to 10 cm in diameter, and are scarlet red in colour. This species is getting to be rare, and it is listed as an endangered species. One of its characteristic features is its reflexed filaments.

Hibiscus brackenridgei
This species is also a native of Hawaii. In growth forms it varies from sprawling shrubs to large trees. A distinct characteristic of this species is its pronounced pubescence. The flowers are bright yellow, each measuring about 7.5 to 12 cm in diameter.

Hibiscus youngianus

A native species of Hawaii, this grows normally to a shrub but sometimes to a small tree. It is known as a native pink, and also for its sterility. For this reason, it is not used for hybridizing. However, it is a prolific seeder. The flowers are lavender in colour, and range from 7.5 to 10 cm in diameter.

Wilder's White
Hibiscus arnottianus

This is one of the well-known Hawaiian native species, and from this species many horticultural varieties have been produced. In growth habits it varies from a shrub to a small tree, growing to a height of 3 to 8 m. The shrub is lovely, with beautiful and fragrant white flowers. It has a characteristic long, red staminal column, with slender stamens rising at the top half of the column up to 15 cm long. The flowers are fairly large, measuring 10 to 15 cm in diameter. The species flowers freely, and sets seeds. It may therefore be grown from seeds, but 15 cm cuttings of pencil thickness will root readily in coarse sand. It grows well in an open sunny situation, with rich sandy soil.

Hibiscus arnottianus

HIBISCUS HYBRIDS

6 Hibiscus Hybrids

Today, the forms of hibiscus are very variable in their blooms, leaves, shapes, and habit. This is because of the growing interest in the past forty years, which have resulted in the development of many new varieties all over the world, estimated at over a thousand. The flower ranges in form from single, semi-double, and double petal. The colours are basically white, pink, red, salmon, orange, yellow, lavender to purplish, and multicoloured. Many varieties are composed of shades of two or more colours.

The recent interest in breeding hybrids has resulted in some confusion in relation to the correct origin and name of many varieties. Each crossing between two species or varieties will result in a few to 20 seeds. The progeny from seeds are variable, and differ from their parents. Each seed can become a variety, and can be vegetatively propagated. It is desirable to advise all breeders and nurserymen to discard those varieties which do not deserve to be propagated, and to standardize the naming of each variety. There is a great tendency for a variety to be called by different names in different places. A central place of registration and reference should be located in a Hibiscus Society, Botanical Garden, or government research institute.

Hybridizing Hibiscus

The hybridization of hibiscus was started over a century ago in Chelsea, England. This was followed by the work of people in Hawaii and Florida in the early twentieth century. But it was not until after World War II that the increased interest in the hybridizing of hibiscus resulted in many new varieties, with emphasis on better quality in foliage as well as growth habits, and a better combination of colours in the blooms. This is the aim of hybridizers who strive to improve on older varieties, but one has to have definite reasons for crossing two varieties, such as for better colour, disease or pest resistance or shape of blooms. When crossing two varieties, we have to be careful to select the right parents so as to produce the desired combination of colours of the cross. In hybridizing hibiscus there are certain procedures to follow.

One must remember that hybrids are of mixed ancestors, and that many types will result from a cross, so that a seed need not come true to type, that is, reproduce itself identically. A few resulting hybrids may be superior to the parents, and the majority may be inferior, so that the best seedlings with the desirable characteristics are selected and the rest destroyed. The selected hybrids can then be named, and subsequently vegetatively propagated.

Siti Hasmah

    The hibiscus flowers can be self-pollinated, which is done by putting the pollen from the anthers of the flower to the stigma of the same flower, while cross-pollination is carried out by using two different plants, one to supply the pollen and the other to receive it. In order to do the crossing, the stigma, or female part, must be ready to receive the pollen. This is indicated by signs of stickiness on the stigmatic lobes. At this point the pollen from the male parent is placed on the stigma of the female parents. If the cross has been successful the fruit is formed and will set seeds. The flower is tagged with the names of both the parents. As the fruit matures, it will turn brown in colour. The number of seeds varies from a few to twenty per fruit. The seed size also varies from that of an okra seed to that of a pea. The seeds are greyish to brown in colour, and some are hairy. Seeds can be kept for a few weeks after drying, but it is recommended to plant them as soon as possible.

    Seeds for planting may have to be treated, or scarified, for quicker germination. Apply moist heat at around 40°C for a few days prior to sowing. An alternative method is to soak the seeds overnight in warm water.

Jol Wright

The Path

Drain the seeds, and plant them in good garden soil, peat, or sand, and keep them moist. They should germinate within two to four weeks. These seedlings are then transplanted into polybags and put in the shade, and are gradually transferred to sunny location. They can be later transplanted again into large pots, and fertilized regularly. The plants raised from the seeds will take eight to sixteen months to bloom. During the growing period the habits of each of these plants have to be observed and noted, i.e., the branching, foliage, growth rate. Finally we come to the exciting part, which is the bloom. These blooms from the same cross have to be compared, and they have to be rated with similar ones already in the market. If they are not showing any improvements they should not be used. Only the outstanding blooms are to be recorded, with a colour slide to show proof of their beauty. This is the reward for hybridizing hibiscus, and the cross can then be named and registered as a new hybrid, to be added to the many hundreds of varieties. The new hybrids are usually named after the breeder or family, such as Isobel Beard, and very often they are named after dignitaries, such as John F. Kennedy.

Scarlet Giant

Clan McEilvary

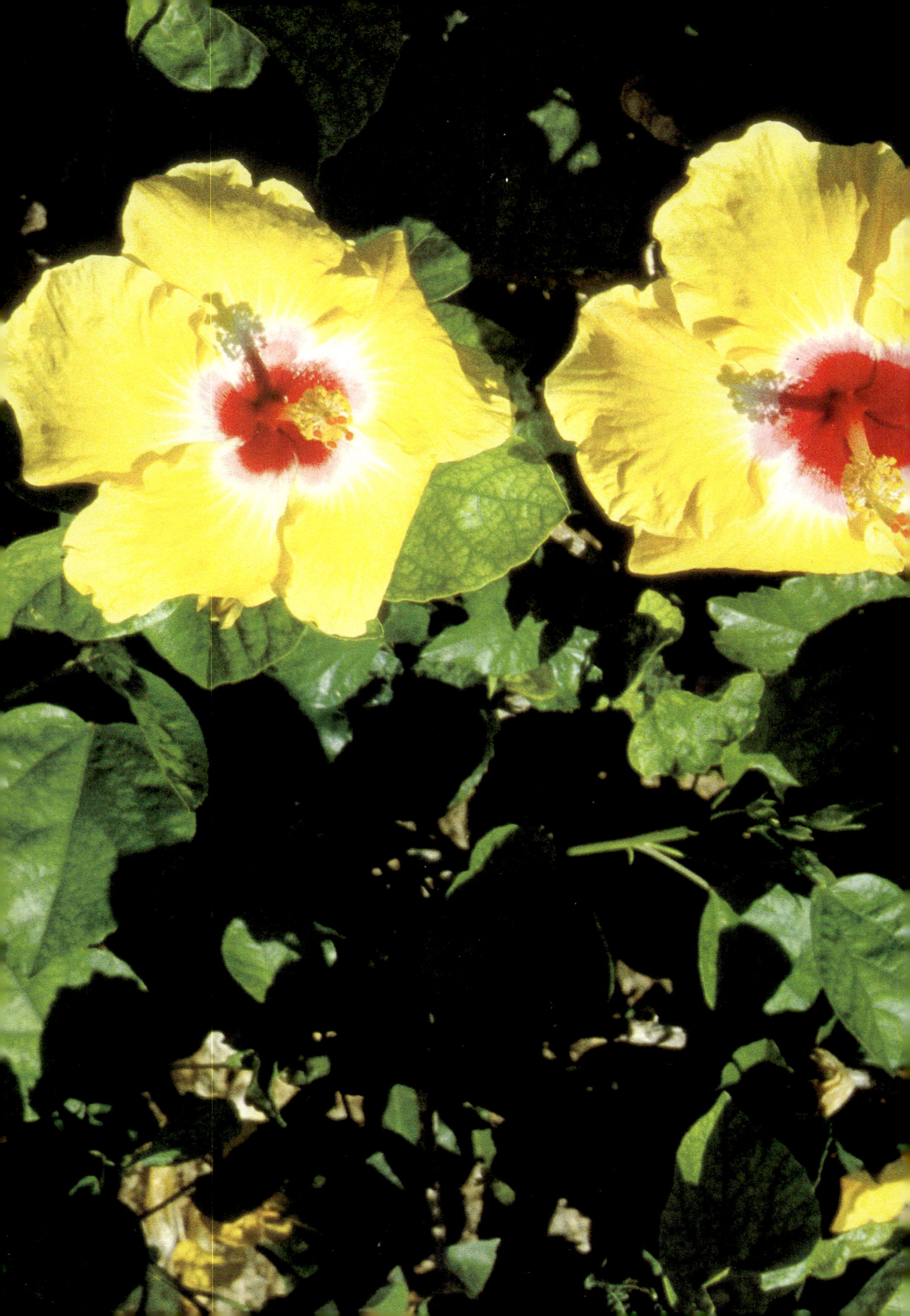

Meteor

All Aglow × *Nathan Charles*

Norman Lee

Natal

Joan Kinchen

Inex Andrew

Gina Marie

Norman Lee × *All Aglow*

Duplex

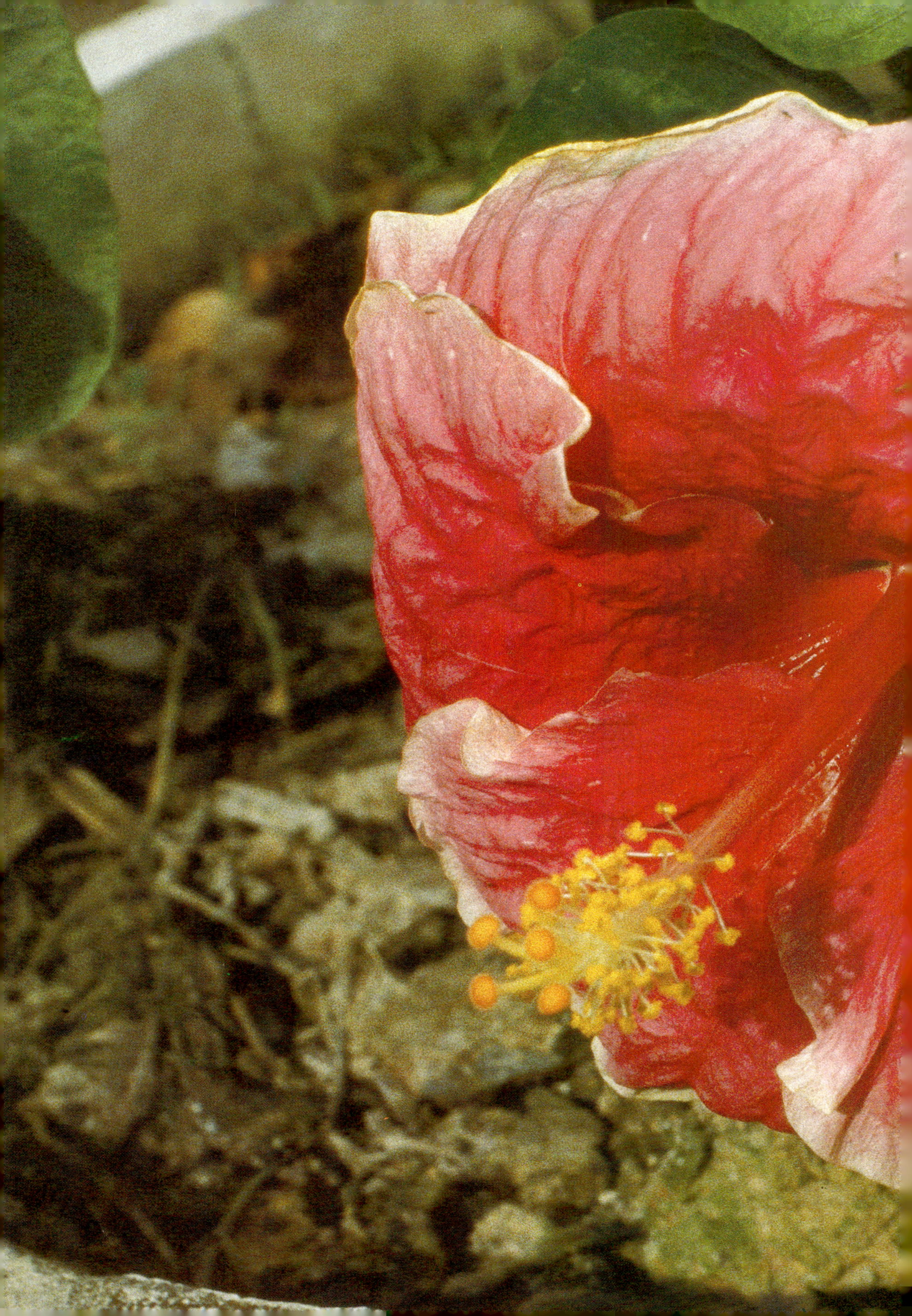

Red Parasol

Madonna

John F. Kennedy

Powder Puff

Cele Niffenegger

Pink Wings

Norma

Jan McIntyre

Insignus

Kissed

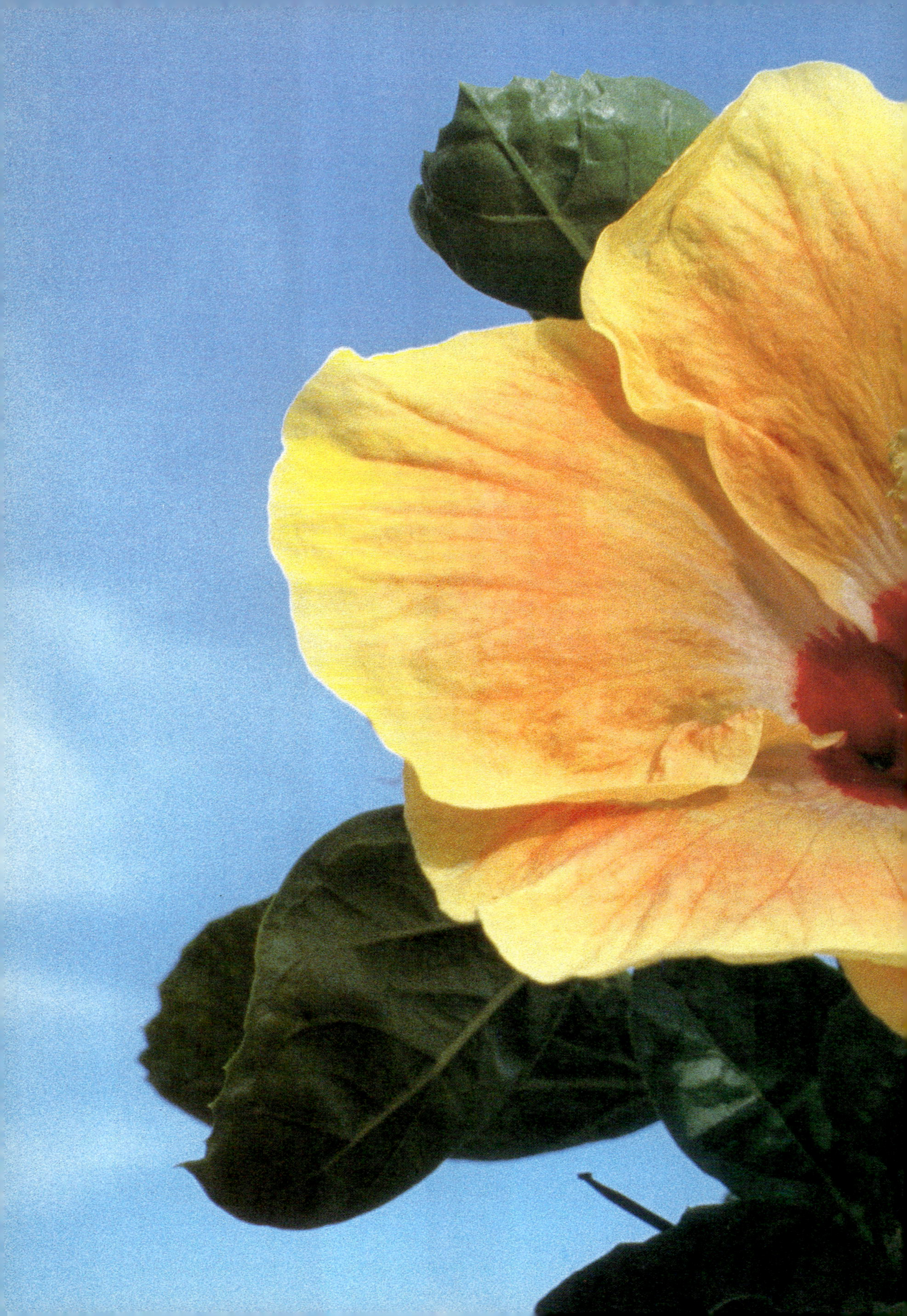

Hawaiian Girl

Christopher Howie

Freddie Brubaker

Lucky Me × *Cherry Smash*

Wilmae

La France

Vasco

Orchid White

Baby Blue

Raindrop × Bride

Flame of Rio

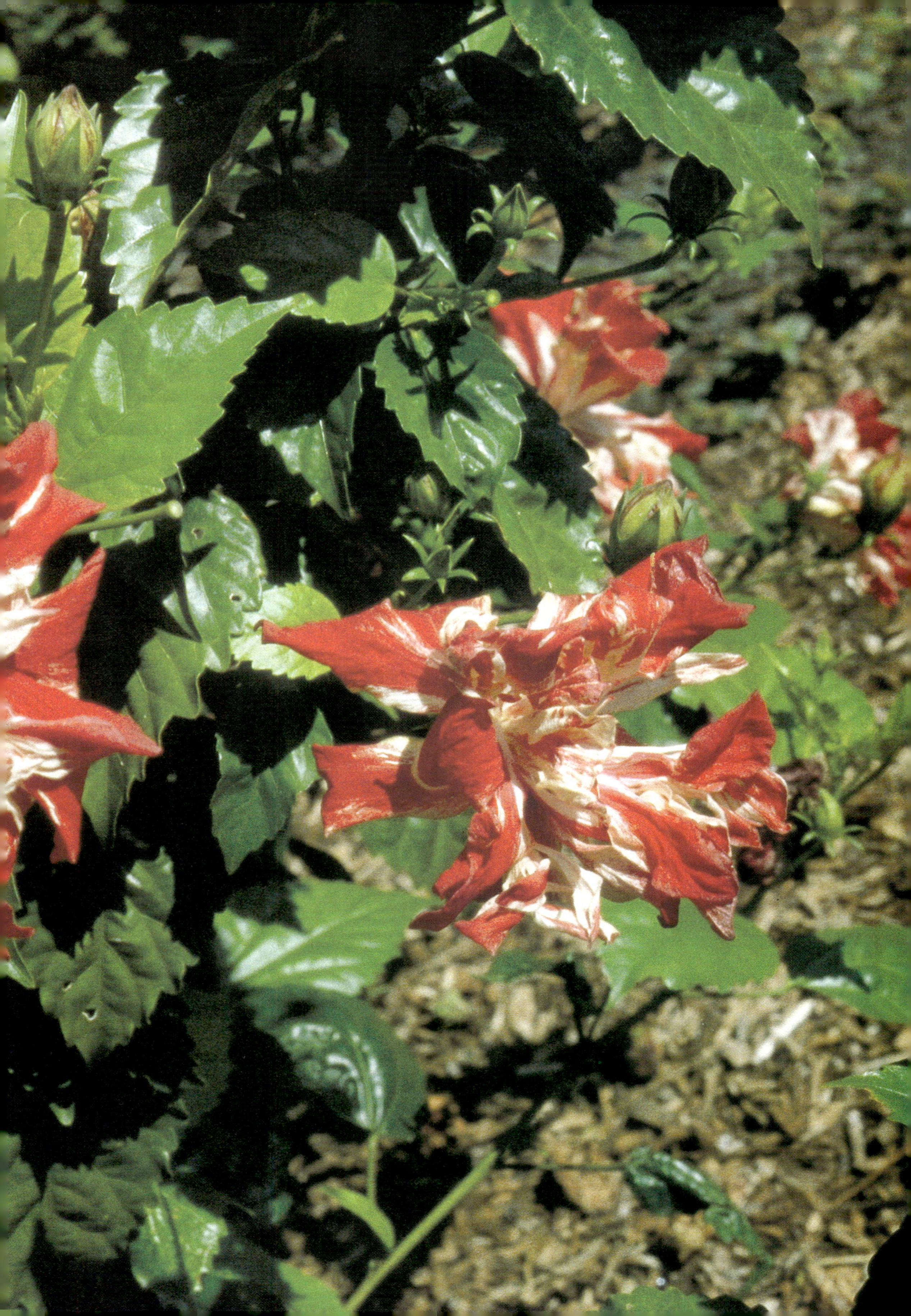

Hula Girl

Evening Sunset

Lady Cilento

Isobel Beard

Pink Rays

Nathan Charles

Mandy Lee

Carrie Ann

Crimson Ray

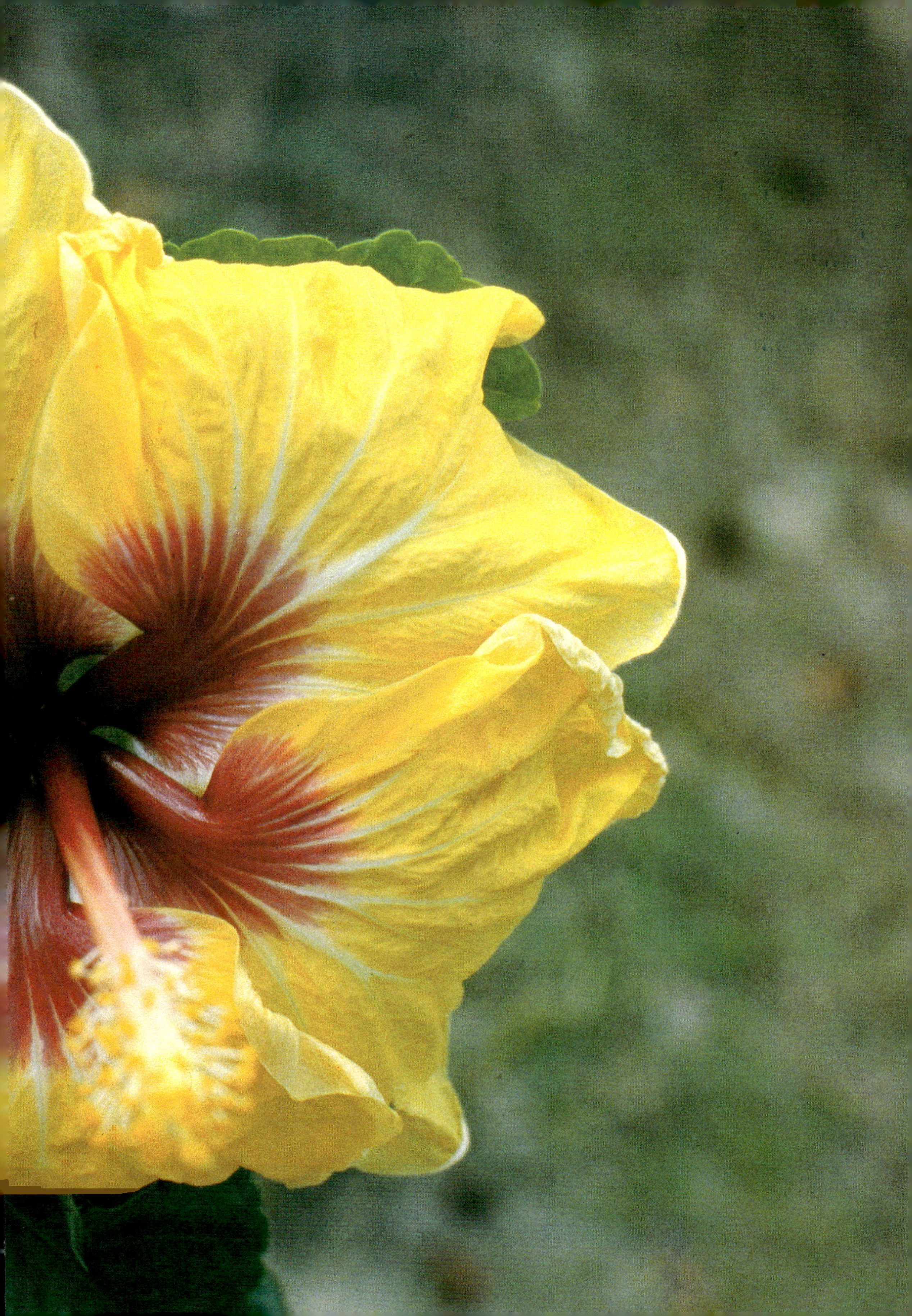

Firedance

Linda Pearl

Mini Skirt

Exquisite

Colleen Hava

Red Beret

Mary Brady

Maya On Red

Charles Dixon

Punta Gorda Gold

Ritt 470

Single Red

Fijian Island

Seminole Pink

Single Orange

President

Fijian White

Orange Eye

Chitra

Coconut Ice

Capitolio

Single Yellow

Sweet Heart

Peggy Walton

Aurora

Black Prince

Geaker of Baroda

Percy Lancaster

PROPAGATION, PLANTING AND MAINTENANCE

7 Propagation, Planting, and Maintenance

Hibiscus, or Bunga Raya, produces seeds only in certain regions of the tropics, but do not set seeds in Malaysia, hence they can be propagated here only by vegetative means. In places like Hawaii, Florida, and Queensland they set seeds, therefore they can be propagated by seeds in those places. For hibiscus to set seeds, the weather has to be drier and cooler than the wet humid tropics. In general, hibiscus may be propagated by seeds, stem cuttings, marcotting or air-layering, budding, and grafting.

Seeds

Propagation by seeds is used mainly to produce new varieties, and the method is therefore used by plant breeders. The reason for this is that seeds do not produce seeds which are true to type. To produce many plants of the same variety, vegetative means (cuttings, grafting, or marcotting) have to be used.

The process of seed propagation involves pollination and fertilization. To bring them from seeds to flowering plants takes a period of twelve to eighteen months. Pollination is the transfer of pollen to the stigma of the flower. This can be self-pollination, if within the same flower, or cross-pollination if it involves another flower. Early in the morning, anthers are removed from the flower by cutting off petals with scissors before the flower opens. Bag the entire bud with a cellophane or paper bag. The following morning, remove the bag, and pollinate the stigmatic lobes, and bag the bud again for a period of one to two days until the stigmas have withered. Pollination is carried out in the morning between 8 and 11 a.m. The best period for pollinating the plant is when they are vigorously producing flowers. On successful pollination and fertilization, seed pods ripen in five to seven weeks. The bagged pods can then be harvested. The number of seeds vary from a few to about 20 per pod. After seed treatment, they can be sown in a seed box. The seedling growth and performance have to be observed till flowering. Their quality is assessed, and a new variety can then be registered.

Cuttings

Many varieties of hibiscus are easily propagated vegetatively by cuttings of different types. Softwood cuttings are common; tip cuttings of half-ripened wood that is still green at the tip are best materials for propagation. These

Stem cuttings in pot

Rooted cuttings

will also give an upright growth, producing a standard plant. These cuttings will produce roots within four to six weeks even without the application of rooting hormones. The successfully rooted cuttings will produce flowers within a few months. Mature woody cuttings can also be used; such cuttings having a diameter of a pencil or even larger are also used. They produce plants with a few axillary branches as compared to tip cuttings, which mainly grow terminally, giving a single unbranched stem.

Cuttings grown in polybags

PLATE 7.1   *Propagation by cuttings*

PLATE 7.2 *Stages in marcotting*—*Left:* *Bark removed between incisions*
Centre: *Barkless band is covered with a clay mixture*
Right: *Marcot ready for planting*

Rooted cuttings from the propagation unit, or box, or pot, are then transplanted into individual pots, or large polybags. Hibiscus cuttings root very easily and readily without much special attention. Stick the cuttings in sand or soil media, in a pot or box kept under shade, and water regularly to keep them moist (Plate 7.1). After four to six weeks they can be transplanted into polybags or pots individually.

Marcotting or Air-layering

This particular method is used for varieties which are difficult to root by ordinary stem cuttings. Marcotting can be done at any time of the year, but preferably during a period of active growth For temperate countries, this is between spring- and summer-time. In marcotting, a straight branch is selected, with the diameter of a pencil. Larger ones can also be used. Two incisions are made right round the branch, the distance between being twice the diameter of the branch. The bark between the two incisions is completely removed, and then the cambium is scraped. The barkless band is then covered with a clay mixture made from a ball of about 8 cm in diameter. The clay mixture is then covered with a polythene sheet. Then it is tied above and below the clay mixture (Plate 7.2). After one to three months, roots can be found in the clay mixture. When sufficient roots are produced, the branch is cut off below the marcot. The marcot is then planted after the removal of the polythene covering, taking care not to disturb the root-filled ball of clay. The potted marcotted plant is put in a

PLATE 7.3 *Stages in bud grafting*

sheltered place. After the marcot has been fully established, it can then be planted in the field.

Budding and Grafting

For these two techniques we need to start off with a stock plant, i.e., the plant which we are going to bud or graft on, using the desired variety offered to it as scion. These rootstocks have an influence on the growth of the grafted variety. It is essential to select a vigorous rootstock, as many varieties have benefitted by budding or grafting to a strong rootstock.

PLATE 7.4   *Stages in grafting—Left: Making an oblique incision*
Centre: Scionwood is inserted
Right: Scionwood tied to rootstock

For example, in Malaysia, the common red hibiscus is often used as a rootstock, as it is adaptable, vigorous, and tolerant to injury by some root-knot and rot fungus. The rootstock is propagated by cuttings, which when rooted, placed in pots, are grafted or budded with the desired variety or hybrid.

Budding

Various types of budding, such as shield and patch budding, can be used. For shield budding, an inverted T incision is made in the rootstock 5 to 8 cm from the ground. The bud from the budwood of the desired variety is cut in the form of a shield about an inch long, and it is inserted in the incision made in the rootstock. After insertion, the bud is tied in place with polythene strips or budding tape. When the bud has taken, the tape is removed and the bud allowed to grow, and later the rootstock above the bud is cut off, and only the new bud is allowed to grow into the desired plant (Plate 7.3).

Grafting

The principle is similar to budding, which is to bring together the cambium tissues of the rootstock and the scion to unite to form a continuous conducting system. In grafting, instead of a single bud, a piece of scionwood is used. Hibiscus can be grafted all the year round. Select, as scionwood, a twig or stem of mature wood, and also a compatible rootstock. The procedure for grafting is quite simple. The scionwood should preferably be of the same diameter as the rootstock to ensure a good fit. A common technique used is the side-wedge type. Start by making an oblique incision 10 cm from the base of the rootstock. The cut should not be so deep as to pass

Hibiscus seeds

Hibiscus seedlings

PLATE 7.5   *Seeds and seedlings*

the centre of the stock. Then sharpen the scionwood into a wedge at the basal end. Next, bend the rootstock slightly away from the cut, and insert the wedge-shaped scionwood into the cut. Carefully examine the bark of both scionwood and rootstock to make sure that they are in close contact. Finally, bind the union tightly with a piece of polythene tape (Plate 7.4).

After the buds on the scionwood have sprouted and have grown 5 to 10 cm, the top of the rootstock above the union has to be removed. The grafted plant is allowed to grow, and is later transplanted into large pots or into the ground. The grafted hibiscus will produce blooms within a few months. Initially the blooms are small, and they remain so until they are fully established.

PLANTING

Raising Seedlings

Seeds are usually not planted in a place where they are to be grown permanently. It is a normal practice to raise plants from seedlings in a nursery, and then to transplant them at a later stage in the garden. This is necessary because seedlings need extra care. When they become more hardy they can withstand field conditions better.

In raising seedlings, the seeds are usually sown in a seed box measuring 45 cm square and 10 cm deep. An alternative method is to use a 10-cm-deep round pot of 45 cm diameter. The box or pot is filled with a mixture containing 2 parts of garden or jungle soil, 2 parts of decomposed compost, and 1 part of sand. The mixture is gently made firm and level with the aid of a flat piece of wood. The seed box is then ready to receive the seeds.

Hibiscus seeds may be difficult to germinate as some are quite hard. Prior to sowing they must be either treated with moist heating, or scarified by scratching the seed coat with a knife blade to force early and uniform germination. These treated seeds are then ready for sowing in the seed box. Seeds are sown in a seed box or pot, the size of either depending upon the number of seeds. Normally, seeds from a single fruit, or from a cross between two varieties, are sown in the same box or pot. The seeds are sown on the surface of the soil and are then covered with sand, and the box or pot placed in a shady place to enable the seeds to germinate. When the seedlings have grown to 3 to 8 cm in height, they can be transplanted into individual black polythene bags containing soil rich in organic matter (Plate 7.5). These seedlings are kept in the shade for a few weeks, and they can then gradually be moved to full sunlight till they reach a height of about 25 cm. They can then be transplanted again into larger pots or into open ground. They will come to flower in 12 to 18 months.

Establishing Hibiscus in the Garden

Hibiscus plants are planted out in the open as individuals, as groups, or as hedges. As in the planting of any perennial ornamental shrub or tree, a special planting hole is necessary, whether the plants are grown from a seedling, a bud-grafted rootstock, or a marcot. A hole, preferably a metre square and half a metre deep, is dug. If the soil is poor, it is advisable to replace it with garden soil. A bucketful of organic matter, such as cow dung, chicken dung, or compost, is mixed with the garden soil, and a few hundred grams of fertilizer can be included. The hole is then filled with this mixture. The plant in the pot or bag is first watered a few hours before planting in the garden. A small hole is then dug in the prepared planting area, deep enough to take the bagged plant. The plant is then carefully removed from the pot or bag. In the case of the plastic bag, a cut is made, and the plant is lifted out carefully and placed erect in the hole. The hole is filled with soil and the soil then compacted. The plant is tied to a stake. The soil is covered with mulch, or well-rotted leaves (Fig. 7.1). The plant is watered, and preferably shade is initially provided. The newly-planted plant is watered daily if there is no rain. When it is established, with a few new leaves emerging, the shade can be removed.

When planting in groups, the process is the same as for an individual plant but on a larger scale. Most hibiscus are quite hardy plants, and in large-scale planting along highways, the same standards need not be observed as those for an individual plant in a private garden. As for the establishment of hedges, a long trench, 30 cm wide, is dug alongside the fence. The soil preparation is similar to that for individual plants. In this case rooted cuttings, or plants in polybags, are used as planting materials. The rooted cuttings can be planted 1 m apart in a straight row alongside the fence. In group planting, a space of 1.2–1.35 m between plants is necessary. The new plantings have to be watered regularly until they are established.

A planting hole is dug

Hole is filled with soil mixture

Small hole is dug in planting area

Plant is lowered into hole

Plant is tied to a stake

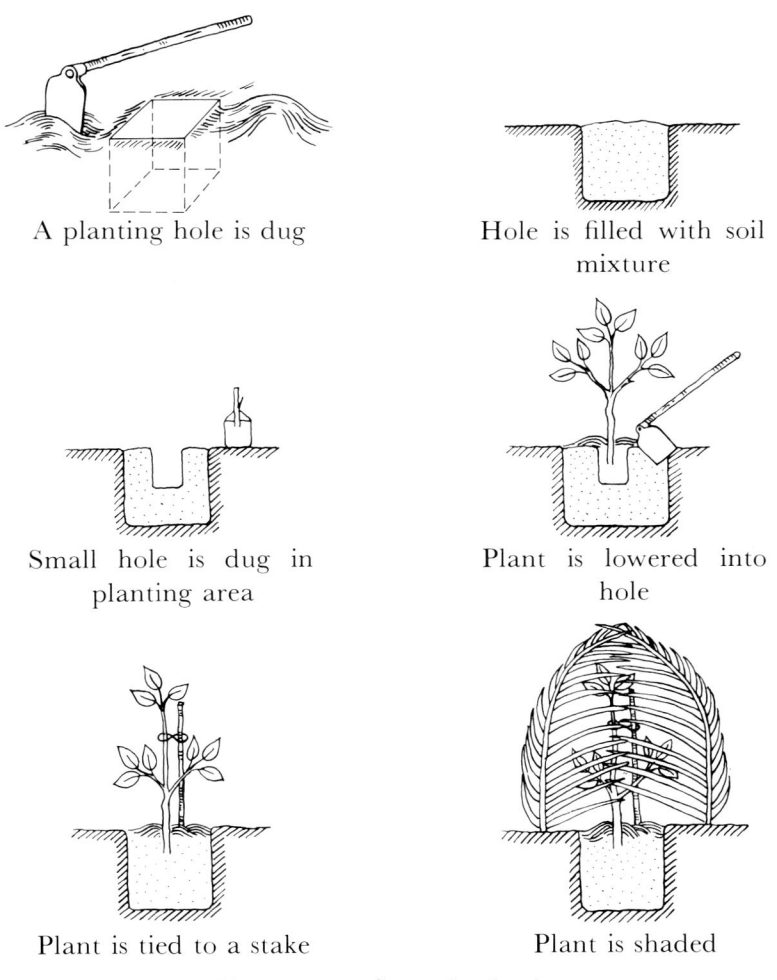

Plant is shaded

Figure 7.1 *Stages in planting*

MAINTENANCE

Like all other ornamental plants, hibiscus has to be maintained carefully after planting, so that it always looks its best, and the gardener can be proud of the quality of his or her plants. The best variety will not perform well if it is not well looked after. Plants which grow vigorously and flower freely in gardens are mainly the result of a high standard of maintenance. This involves the basic principles of providing the plants with sufficient water, fertilizer, and a favourable environment free of pests and diseases. Different plants have special requirements and preferences. Fortunately, hibiscus is quite an easy plant to grow, but introduced hybrids may face some problems of adaptability to the environment and resistance to pests and diseases. Hibiscus plants will usually present an attractive appearance, and will bloom well, if vigorous, healthy growth is encouraged by proper care, which includes cultivation, fertilization, and pest and disease control.

Irrigation or Watering

The hibiscus shrub requires a great amount of water but cannot tolerate water-logged conditions. If there is poor drainage due to soil type, then steps must be taken to drain away excess water, and the cultivator must also make it a point to irrigate regularly, or to water less frequently, i.e., twice a week. When drainage is good, and under dry conditions, watering three to four times a week is necessary. Apply water in shallow basins around the shrub, or in furrows if the shrubs are grown in rows. In the case of pot plants, or any shrub in containers, these require watering daily in the absence of rain.

Cultivation and Weeding

The area around the plant should be kept clear of weeds. This can be done by regular cultivation, to remove weeds as well as lawn grass encroaching into the planting area. Hand weeding with a fork or *cangkul* below the leaf canopy will be sufficient. A contact, general weed-killer can also be used around the plant. In the case of pot plants, hand weeding with a fork, to loosen the soil as well as to remove the weeds, ensures no competition from other plants.

Fertilization

To ensure healthy growth the plants must be given sufficient nutrients. This can come in different forms, such as organic matter and commercial fertilizers. At the very beginning, before the shrub is planted, one must put in lots of organic matter and subsequently keep the plants mulched. In order to promote and maintain vigorous growth, it is essential that they should be fertilized regularly. A suitable compound fertilizer, containing 12% nitrogen, 5% phosphorous, and 14% potash, can be applied regularly. A few tablespoonfuls will be sufficient for a small plant, whereas a small tree may require 250–500 g spread below the leaf canopy once every four to five months. It is preferable to use less fertilizer, but fertilize more frequently, using a balanced fertilizer. It has been found that potash is very good for flowering in hibiscus and to obtain good blooms. Use about 100 g of potassium sulphate in 20 L of water, and apply one cup to each mature plant. The amount to be applied and the frequency depend on the age and size of the plants. Organic fertilizer, like cow dung or chicken dung, is beneficial to the plants as well as improving the soil. Other organic fertilizers, containing blood and bone, are good, but the nutrients are not readily available to the plants.

Pruning

In the tropics, due to favourable growing seasons all year round, there is no definite pruning schedule to be set, unlike the situation in the temperate regions. It also depends on the type of pruning, whether it is formative, or routine removal of weak twigs, or severe pruning of old shrubs with numerous bare branches. In the case of formative pruning, to achieve a single stem standard, all the side shoots are removed when the plant has reached the desired height, and the top is then pinched to induce branches. In the case of vigorous plants, light pruning is done to the shoots, so as to prevent a leggy appearance to the plant. For older shrubs with lots of bare branches, the plant is severely pruned and dead twigs and small branches are removed at the same time. For hedge hibiscus, the top and the sides are pruned to keep the hedge tidy and straight.

After pruning, it is advisable to fertilize the plants with a complete fertilizer or with manure. It is best to accompany this by a light cultivation around the trunk or stem of the plant, followed by thorough watering. Within a few weeks new growth will appear, forming a new healthy plant.

Pest and Disease Control

The common hibiscus is quite a hardy plant and relatively free from pest attack. However, the introduced hybrids may be more susceptible to pests and diseases, especially during the rainy season. The few insects that sometimes attack hibiscus are some sucking and chewing insects, mites, aphids, and scale insects. They are found on the stem, twigs, and leaves. The flower and leaf buds can also be attacked by stink bug.

These insect pests can be controlled by a spray containing either Malathion (two teaspoonfuls per gallon of water), or with oil added, to control scale insects. Some varieties do not accept this spray, and using it on them results in defoliation. Other useful insecticides are Tamaron for sucking aphids, and Basudin, Dipterex, and Sevin for chewing insects. The dosage for each is recommended on the instruction label.

Hibiscus is also sometimes attacked by root-knot nematode, but most plants are tolerant of this pest. Those grown under a mulch are less severely injured. Another disorder that hibiscus suffers is a nutritional one, showing symptoms of chlorosis of the leaves, and occurring especially in coastal and acid soils. Chelated iron and manganese sulphate can be applied to the soil. A spray containing iron, manganese, and zinc given two or three times a year will improve the condition of the plants.

Flower bud drop is another condition noticeable with hibiscus. Unhealthy plants, infected by insects and nematode, or suffering from nutrient deficiency, will also cause flowers to drop prematurely. A high percentage of nitrogen in the fertilizer has also been reported to have caused bud drop.

References

BEERS, L and HOWIE, J (1985) *Growing Hibiscus*, Kangaroo Press. 88pp.

BHAT, R.M. AND VERMA V.K. (1980). *Morphological descriptions of some new varieties of Hibiscus rosa-sinensis South Indian Horticulture.* 28, 21–23.

BURKILL, I.H. (1986) *A dictionary of the economic products of the Malay Peninsula.* Ministry of Agriculture and Cooperatives, Kuala Lumpur, Malaysia. Vol. 1, 1182–93.

MCCONNELL, L.S. (1950) *The hibiscus—its history, culture and uses.* Tropical Gardening. 1, 20

CRILEY, R. (1980) *Potted flowering hibiscus.* Florida Review. 165, 48–49.

DICKEY, R.D. (1962) *Hibiscus in Florida.* Bulletin 168 A. Florida Agriculture Experiment Station. University of Florida, Gainsville. 32pp.

NAKASONE, H.Y. and RAUCH, F.D. (1980) *Ornamental Hibiscus—Propagation and culture.* Research Bulletin 175—Hawaii Agricultural Experiment Station. 12pp.

PALMER, K. and PALMER, M. (1954) *Hibiscus unlimited and how to know them.* St. Petersburg, Florida. 120pp.

SHANKS, J.B. (1972) *Chemical control of growth and flowering in Hibiscus.* Hortscience 7, 574.

WILKINS, J.F. and KOTECKI, D. (1982) *Hibiscus rosa-sinensis L. The Chinese Hibiscus, Hawaiian hibiscus, rose of China, China rose, blacking plant.* Minnesota State Florist Bulletin 31, 3–7.

Index

A
Air-layering 138, 140
All Aglow × Nathan Charles 72
Alternate 46
Annual 46, 56
Anther sac 12
Antidote 31
Assam Susur 56
Aurora 133
Axil 46

B
Baby Blue 99
Bark 55
Basudin 147
Bendi 31, 46
Black Prince 134
Boats 48
Borders 53
Botanical description 6
Botanical garden 26
Branching 53
Bristly 47
Bronchitis 31
Budding 138, 141, 142
Bunga Raya 16, 40, 42, 43, 44, 138

C
Calendar of Hibiscus 20, 21
Calyx 11, 40
Capitolio 129
Capsules 40, 47
Carrie Ann 109
Carvings 22
Cele Niffenegger 85
Changeable Rose 27
Charles Dixon 119
Chinese Hibiscus 6, 40
Chinese Rose 40

Chitra 127
Chlorosis 147
Christopher Howie 92
Clan McEilvary 69
Coconut Ice 128
Colleen Hava 116
Compost 144
Container plant 27
Coral Hibiscus 50
Cordage 48
Corolla 40
Cough 31
Crimson Ray 110, 111
Cross pollination 65
Cultivation 146
Cuttings 48, 50, 51, 53, 54, 58, 138, 139

D
Deciduous 51
Decoction 31
Dipterex 147
Disease 147
Dissected 50
Double form 10
Drinks 56
Duplex 79
Dyeing 43

E
Ear-aches 31
Epicalyx 8, 11, 40
Erect 46, 47, 56
Evening Sunset 103
Evergreen 40, 48
Exquisite 115
Eyebrows 2, 43

F
Fertilizer 146, 147
Fertilization 138, 146
Fever 31

Fibre 48, 55
Fijian Island 122
Fijian White 126
Filament 8, 59
Fingerprints 40
Firedance 2, 112
Flame of Rio 100, 101
Floral decoration 33
Flower arrangement 32, 38
Flower decorations 27
Flower forms 10
Flower shapes 9
Food 31
Forest 40, 55
Foyer 27
Freddie Brubaker 93
Fruits 40, 46, 65
Funnel 9

G
Garlands 48
Geaker of Baroda 135
Germinate 40, 67
Germination 65
Gina Marie 77
Glabrous 56
Grafting 138, 141, 142
Group planting 28
Growth 48, 59
Growth forms 7

H
Hawaiian Girl 90, 91
Headache 31
Hedges 26, 29
Hibiscus City 26
   description 8
   flower 11
   Garden 26
   girl 37
   hybrids 63, 64

shrub 7
standard plants 34, 43
seed 13
species 39, 40
Hibiscus abelmoschus 31, 47
  acetosella 58
  arnottianus 61, 62
  brackenridgei 60
  cannabinus 31
  elatus 16
  esculentus 9, 31, 46
  kokio 59
  macrophyllus 31, 55
  manihot 47
  moschentos 54
  mutabilis 31, 44, 45
  rockii 58
  rosa sinensis 6, 9, 16, 40, 42
  sabdariffa 9, 31, 56
  schizopetalus 50
  syriacus 51
  tiliaceus 31, 48
  youngianus 61
Hibiscus variety
  All Aglow × Nathan Charles 72
  Aurora 133
  Baby Blue 99
  Black Prince 134
  Capitolio 129
  Carrie Ann 109
  Cele Niffenegger 85
  Charles Dixon 119
  Chitra 127
  Christopher Howie 92
  Clan McEilvary 69
  Coconut Ice 128
  Colleen Hava 116
  Crimson Ray 110, 111
  Duplex 79
  Evening Sunset 103
  Exquisite 115
  Fijian Island 122
  Fijian White 126
  Firedance 2, 112
  Flame of Rio 100, 101
  Freddie Brubaker 93
  Geaker of Baroda 135
  Gina Marie 77
  Hawaiian Girl 90, 91
  Hula Girl 102
  Insignus 89
  Isobel Beard 2, 67, 105
  Jan McIntyre 88
  Joan Kinchen 75
  John F. Kennedy 2, 67, 83
  Jol Wright 66
  Kissed 89
  Lady Cilento 104
  La France 96
  Linda Pearl 113
  Lucky Me × Cherry Smash 94
  Madonna 82
  Mandy Lee 108
  Mary Brady 118
  Maya On Red 119
  Meteor 70, 71
  Mini Skirt 2, 114
  Natal 74
  Norma 87
  Norman Lee 73
  Norman Lee × All Aglow 78
  Orange Eye 126
  Orchid White 98
  Peggy Walton 132
  Percy Lancaster 136
  Pink Rays 106, 107
  Pink Wings 86
  Powder Puff 84
  President 125
  Punta Gorda Gold 120
  Raindrop × Bride 99
  Red Beret 117
  Red Parasol 80, 81
  Ritt 470, 120
  Scarlet Giant 68
  Seminole Pink 123
  Single Orange 124
  Single Red 121
  Single Yellow 130
  Siti Hasmah 65
  Snow Flake 7
  Sweet Heart 2, 131
  The Path 67
  Vasco 97
  Wilder's White 61
  Wilmae 95
Highway 26, 30
History 6
Horticultural 61
Hula Girl 102
Hybridising 61, 64

I
Industrial use 31
Inex Andrew 76
Insignus 89
Irrigation 146
Isobel Beard 2, 67, 105

J
Jan McIntyre 88
Japanese Lantern 50
Joan Kinchen 75
John F. Kennedy 2, 67, 83
Jol Wright 66
Jungles 55

K
Kapas Hutan 47
Key rings 22
Kissed 89

L
Lady Cilento 104
Lady's Finger 8, 46
La France 96
Landscaping 26, 27
Lanterns 50
Leaves 31
Linda Pearl 113
Loams 46
Lobes 50
Lounge 27
Lowland 55
Lucky Me × Cherry Smash 94

M
Madonna 82
Maintenance 138, 145
Malathion 147
Malvaviscus conzatii 53
Mandy Lee 108
Marcotting 43, 50, 140
Mary Brady 118
Maya On Red 119
Medicinal Use 31
Medicine 43
Medium 55
Meteor 70, 71
Mini Skirt 2. 114
Musk seed 47
Musk Mallow 47
Musky 47
Mulch 147

N
Natal 74
National Flower 16
Nematodes 147
Nomenclature 2

Norma 87
Norman Lee 73
Norman Lee × All Aglow 78

O
Oblique 142
Oil 46, 56
Okra 8, 9, 31, 46
Ornamental 26, 40, 43, 50, 51
Orange Eye 126
Orchid White 98

P
Painting 24
Parks 30
Patios 27
Peduncles 56
Peggy Walton 132
Pendulous 50
Percy Lancaster 136
Perennial 54, 144
Pest 147
Petals 11, 50
Petioles 56
Pink Rays 106, 107
Pink Wings 86
Planting 138, 144
Pods 138
Pollen grain 8, 12
Pollen sac 8
Pollination 138
Polybags 140, 145
Potted plants 27, 35, 43
Powder Puff 84
President 125
Propagation 138
Pruning 147
Pubescence 60
Pukoonis 59
Punta Gorda Gold 120

R
Raindrop × Bride 99
Red Beret 117
Red-leaf Hibiscus 58
Red Parasol 80, 81
Red Sorrel 56
Reference 64, 148
Reflexed 9, 50
Registration 64
Remedy 31
Ritt 470, 120
Robust 46
Rock's Hibiscus 58
Rooted cuttings 139, 140
Roots 31
Rootstock 141, 142, 144
Ropes 55
Rose of China 2
Roselle 56
Rose Mallow 54
Rose of Sharon 27
Roundabouts 26
Rukun Negara 16, 22

S
Salt resistant 48
Saucer 9
Scarified 40, 65
Scarlet Giant 68
Scionwood 142, 143
Sea Hibiscus 48
Seeds 13, 54, 58, 65, 138
Self-pollinated 65
Semidouble form 10
Seminole Pink 123
Sevin 147
Shoe flower 40, 42, 43
Shrub 40, 51, 53, 56, 58
Single form 10
Single Orange 124
Single Red 121
Single Specimen plant 36

Single Yellow 130
Siti Hasmah 65
Snow Flake 7
Sowing 40, 65
Stamens 8, 11, 40
Staminal column 8, 11
Stem cuttings 43, 139
Sterility 61
Stigma 11, 65
Style 50
Sweet Heart 2, 131
Syrian Ketrina 51

T
Tamaron 147
The Path 67
Timber 55
Timun Hibiscus 48
Toys 55
Tree Hibiscus 48
Tropical 58
Turk's Cap 53
Tutor 55

U
Uses 26

V
Variations 51
Varieties 138
Vasco 97
Vegetables 40, 46

W
Waimea Arboretum 26
Watering 146
Wedge 143
Weeding 146
Weed killer 146
Wilder's White 61
Wilmae 95
Wind 48
Wood 138